THE CHURCH UNDER THE SHADOW OF SHARIAH:

A CHRISTIAN ASSESSMENT

Edited by
John Cheong and Peter Riddell

Occasional Papers in the Study of Islam
No. 6 (2017)

The Arthur Jeffery Centre for the Study of Islam
Melbourne School of Theology

An affiliated college of the Australian College of Theology

Arthur Jeffery Centre for the Study of Islam Occasional Papers
The Church under the Shadow of Shariah: A Christian Perspective
No 6. (2017)
ISSN 1836-9782
ISBN 978-0-9876154-5-9
© 2017 Melbourne School of Theology Press. All rights reserved.

Editors

John Cheong and Peter Riddell

Series Editor

Peter Riddell

Production and Cover Design

Ho-yuin Chan

Publishing Services

Published by Melbourne School of Theology Press

Arthur Jeffery Centre for the Study of Islam
Melbourne School of Theology
5 Burwood Highway, Wantirna, Victoria 3152, Australia.
PO Box 6257, Vermont Sth, Victoria 3133, Australia
Ph: +61 3 9881 7800, Fax: +61 3 9800 0121
info@jefferycentre.mst.edu.au, www.mst.edu.au

People involved in the field of Christian relations with other faiths are welcome to submit related items to the Editor for consideration for publishing in the Arthur Jeffery Centre for the Study of Islam Occasional Papers.

Opinions and conclusions published in the Arthur Jeffery Centre for the Study of Islam Occasional Papers are those of the authors and do not necessarily represent the views of the Editor(s) or the Centre. The Occasional Papers is purely an information medium, to inform interested parties of religious trends, discussions and debates. The Occasional Papers do not intend in any way to actively promote hatred of any religion or its followers.

TABLE OF CONTENTS

INTRODUCTION: OPENING THE DOOR TO SHARIAH
  Prof Peter Riddell 5

PART A: SHARIAH'S ORIGINS AND UNFOLDING IN THE WORLD ... 13
REFLECTIONS ON THE MEANING OF SHARĪ'A
  Dr Olaf Schumann 15
FROM SHARIAH TO SOCIETY: CASE STUDIES FROM EGYPT, PAKISTAN AND INDONESIA
  Prof Peter G Riddell 29
THE IRANIAN CHURCH UNDER THE SHADOW OF SHIA SHARI'AH
  Dr Anthony McRoy 55
THE APPLICATION OF SHARI'A-LAW ENFORCED BY REGIONAL GOVERNMENTS IN INDONESIA
  Dr Olaf Schumann 75
THE CHURCH UNDER THE LENGTHENING SHADOW OF SYARIAH IN BRUNEI DARUSSALAM
  C.T. and Dr John Cheong 91

PART B: CASE STUDIES OF THE CHURCH UNDER THE SHADOW OF SHARIAH IN MALAYSIA 109
THE CHURCH UNDER THE SHADOW OF SHARIAH: EXPLORING DIMENSION AND RESPONSES IN MALAYSIA
  Eugene Yapp 111
THE DEVELOPMENT OF SYARIAH LAW IN MALAYSIA: IMPLICATIONS FOR MUSLIMS AND CHRISTIANS
  Dr John Cheong 143

CONCLUSION: RETROSPECT AND PROSPECTS
  Dr John Cheong 163

CONTRIBUTORS 177
NOTES FOR CONTRIBUTORS 179

Introduction: Opening the door to Shariah

Prof Peter Riddell

In the 21st century, the expression, "Shariah" – as in "Shariah law" and "Shariah finance" or "Islamic banking" – is heard with increasing frequency (Hefner 2011, Sloane-White 2017). It is important to be clear on just what Shariah is, particularly since some Muslim activists are increasingly promoting it around the world.[1]

The prolific Western scholar of Islamic law, Joseph Schacht, once described the Shariah as "the core and kernel of Islam itself" (Schacht, 1974:392). The concept appears obliquely in the Qur'an at verse 45:18: "*Then We put thee on the (right) Way of Religion [Shariah]: so follow thou that (Way), and follow not the desires of those who know not*". This passage underpins the common Muslim claim that Shariah law is divinely sourced, fixed and immutable, a gift to humanity from Allah, designed to show Muslims how to live and govern correctly.

Of course, there are different schools of legal interpretation. By the middle of the eighth century A.D., several had emerged in the Muslim Abbasid Empire. Of these, four survived among majority Sunni Muslims: the Hanafite, Malikite, Shafi'ite, and Hanbalite schools, the last being the most conservative/literalist. Further schools emerged among the minority Shiite Muslims, and several are in play today, as explained in Anthony McRoy's paper on "The Iranian Church under the Shadow of Shi'a Shariah".

Even a cursory look at Shariah legal codes shows that they are marked with **inequality** and **excess**. Consider first, inequality; in Shariah courts, "all jurists, court officials and the judge must be Muslims; non-Muslims are not allowed to take part in any way. No woman may become a judge" (Solomon & Wakeling, 2009: 7).

---

[1] In this volume, the word "shariah" is spelled differently by various authors. Rather than trying to unify them into one standard spelling, we allow each author to express shariah as it is commonly used in their local contexts (e.g., syariah in Brunei and Malaysia, syariat in Indonesia, shari'a in the Middle East and shariah/sharia in Western contexts).

In matters of family law, Shariah law codes draw on the Qur'an (verses 2-3 of chapter 4) to permit polygamy. But only the Muslim male is allowed multiple marriage partners. Furthermore, these Muslim males can choose among Muslim, Jewish, or Christian women, while Muslim women must of necessity choose from their own community of the faithful.

If marriages run into trouble, divorce is far easier for Muslim husbands than for wives. This is clear from the *fiqh* (jurisprudential) texts, which generally understand the husband to be the divorcer, while "there is consensus that the divorcee is the wife" (Maghniyyah, 1995: 383). And when divorce occurs, Muslim wives can easily lose custody of their children. For instance, when children reach the age of seven, custody automatically passes to the father. Then, when Muslim parents die, the cycle of privilege continues, for sons inherit twice as much as daughters.

If a Jewish or Christian woman marries a Muslim, Shariah law determines that the children automatically become Muslim, and according to the consensus, the mother is ineligible to receive an inheritance when her Muslim husband dies. The same goes for a person who leaves the faith (a *murtadd* or apostate), "except if he returns and repents before the distribution of the heritage" (Maghniyyah, 1995: 468). The question of apostasy is considered in some detail in a number of papers in the volume.

Inequality also extends to courtroom procedure. For instance, the testimony of a Muslim carries twice the weight of the witness of a non-Muslim. Furthermore, "In rape cases only a Muslim male witness's evidence is admissible" (Solomon & Wakeling, 2009: 12).

The other striking dimension of Shariah law is its excessiveness, first in prescribing excessive harshness, and second in its excessive attention to detail. The harshness shows itself in the hudud criminal codes, where public floggings, amputation of limbs, and execution by stoning are stipulated for crimes committed. Such codes are under consideration in Aceh, Brunei and Malaysia, as discussed in following papers.

Flogging is prescribed for fornication by unmarried people, while married men and women caught in adultery (and witnessed by four men, or three men and two women, or two men and four women) are liable to be stoned to death. Thieves found guilty are likely to have a limb amputated (reflecting Q 5:38). And most legal schools prescribe death for abandoning Islam. In contrast, apostasy by non-

Muslims is of no interest to Shariah law; thus, in many Muslim locations Muslim authorities actively seek the conversion of non-Muslims to Islam, as can be seen in Malaysia.

Of course, some of this is reminiscent of the Mosaic law, which prescribed death for a number of offenses, including adultery, idolatry, bestiality, and sorcery. And while amputation was not an Old Testament punishment, stoning and lashing were. But Christians understand that those stern standards set the stage for the gospel, underscoring God's holiness as an introduction to His grace. And the Israelite code was theocratic and temporary, not designed for contemporary culture, in which "Caesar" is duly granted the office of retribution. In contrast, Shariah leans heavily towards theocracy, with harsh, state retribution for impiety.

As for its pickiness, Shariah law can make the Pharisees appear mild. For instance, a leading source of Muslim law in Southeast Asia, the Shafi'ite work *Reliance of the Traveller*, declares that if an unrelated boy and girl baby share the same wet nurse, they become "unmarriageable kin" (al-Misri, 1994: 575-577). In this same text, under "Ibn Hajar Haytami's List of Enormities", one finds condemnation for "plucking eyebrows", "not straightening the row of people praying", and "selling ... wood or the like to someone who will make a musical instrument" (al-Misri, 1994: 971, 977). And this is a more moderate expression of Islamic law than that enforced in Afghanistan and Pakistan by the Taliban, whose religious police ensure that "if any music cassette [is] found in a shop, the shopkeeper should be imprisoned and the shop locked" (Rashid, 2010: 248).

If the above portrayal of Shariah law seems bleak and pessimistic, it should be noted that many ordinary Muslims have a jaundiced view of the Islamic legal codes. Surveys of British Muslims suggest that roughly half are opposed to the introduction of aspects of Shariah law in Britain, and some Muslims, such as the reformist group "Muslims against Sharia", have organised themselves into lobby groups to work against influences from Shariah law. If, then, there are Muslim insiders urging caution on the question of Islamic law, non-Muslims should be sceptical when being presented with a sugar-coated version of Shariah.

The papers

This volume grapples with a set of important issues that relate to Shariah Law. This study is timely because of the gradual increase in the influence of Shariah across the world. This is especially the case in certain Muslim-majority countries, but it is also true to some extent in Western societies where Muslim minority activists are advocating for the implementation of aspects of Shariah Law within non-Islamic legal contexts.

In his first paper in the volume, Dr Olaf Schumann provides a series of insightful reflections on the meaning of the term Shariah, its presence within Islamic sacred literature, and the concept of Shariah as divinely-revealed Law. He also considers the historical development of Islamic Law, adding several helpful comparative observations to the Law in Judaism and Christianity.

The next paper is my own contribution, in which I draw on historical developments in three countries – Egypt, Pakistan and Indonesia (with specific reference to the province of Aceh) – to propose an eight-stage process in the rise of Shariah advocacy by Muslim activists. While Egypt and Pakistan are at a similar point on the eight-stage trajectory, Aceh is at an earlier stage, given that the empowerment of Shariah has only taken place in that region during the twenty-first century.

Dr Anthony McRoy then offers a fascinating study of the place of Shariah Law in the Islamic Republic of Iran and the experience of Christians living under it. He considers a broad sweep of Iranian history and the place of Christianity within that history, including the activities of Christian missionary groups. He then discusses at length the experience of Christians living in Iran under the Islamic Republic since 1979, where Shi'a Shariah provides the very structure of the nation's legal system.

In the following paper, Dr Olaf Schumann returns to consider the advance of Shariah within the Indonesian context. He offers a set of powerful arguments against literalist approaches to the Law, as embraced by increasing numbers of Islamist groups, and challenges the view of Shariah as a divine Law, stating clearly that "the Shari'a, like other 'religious laws', are human-made and should be acknowledged as such". Again he provides helpful comparative reflections drawn from Judaism and Christianity.

Discussion of the situation in Indonesia is important, given the weighting of this present volume towards developments in Southeast Asia. As the largest Muslim country in the world with a population of around 240 million (being eighty eight percent Muslim), pressure for the implementation of Shariah Law in different parts of Indonesia is of considerable significance for both regional and world Islam. When Indonesia gained its independence, the decision not to include the Jakarta Charter in the Constitution – which would have prescribed Shariah Law for Muslim citizens – left a lasting legacy of resentment among many Muslims (Effendy 2003: 33).

In the period of political reform in Indonesia since the fall of President Suharto in 1998, advocates for Shariah empowerment have made a number of gains. The case of the province of Aceh is discussed in my own paper. Elsewhere, Shariah activists have taken full advantage of Indonesian legislation passed since 1998 that favours decentralisation, and gives local communities more autonomy. In one of the more notorious examples, in 2001 Indonesian police arrested Ja'far Umar Thalib, the leader of the radical group *Laskar Jihad*, on a charge of assembling a makeshift Islamic court that led to the death by stoning of an accused rapist. Ja'far was accused of personally leading the execution. Although stoning is illegal under Indonesian law, Ja'far was never prosecuted.[2]

Following the fall of President Suharto, the notorious Islamic Defenders Front (*Front Pembela Islam* - FPI) was established by Habib Mohammad Riziq Shihab. The FPI motto was "Live honourably or die a martyr" (Jamhari 2003: 11).[3] It has carried out campaigns against what it identified as "sites of immorality" in Jakarta and other locations in Indonesia. More recently the FPI was a key player in mass protests against former Jakarta Governor Basuki Tjahaja "Ahok" Purnama, who was charged with blasphemy for accusing his opponents of misinterpreting a Qur'an verse in their campaign against him. Islamist activist groups such as FPI are on the march in their (so far unsuccessful) push for the implementation of Shariah across Indonesia.

The next paper moves the discussion from Indonesia to Brunei. The authors, C.T. and Dr John Cheong, present the paradox of this small and rich Sultanate nation: on the one hand, it is extremely modern and prosperous because of oil revenue, with citizens benefitting from free health care and education, highly subsidised living expenses and other ways that are unique in the region; on the other hand the Sultanate is in the middle of a process of redefining

---

[2] Andreas Harsono, "Profile: Jafar Umar Thalib", *BBC News Online*, 9 May 2002.

[3] "Hidup mulia atau mati syahid".

the legal system to adhere to the dictates of Shariah, with laws that date from medieval contexts. Even though tiny, Brunei is a nation that is now setting the pace or model for other Islamists in Southeast Asia in the process of implementing Shariah laws. Thus, how it navigates this paradox in light of the harshness of its punishments and the plight of its minority non-Muslim population under Shariah law (that seems helpless to retard its progress) versus its desire to be globally respected as a modern nation bears watching.

The final two substantive papers consider the situation in Malaysia, where pressure to increase the role of Shariah Law has been evident for several decades. A lawyer by profession, Eugene Yapp traces the process of empowerment of Shariah courts and rising Shariah legislation. He then considers the impact on the church of expanded and strengthened Shariah jurisdiction, including hudud laws which, in spite of assurances to the contrary, have affected non-Muslims to an increased degree. He offers important reflections on how the churches can respond in a climate of creeping Shariah. Eugene Yapp also includes three helpful appendices, listing the many Shariah enactments in recent decades.

In the final substantive paper, Dr John Cheong first considers the historical implementation of Shariah laws and the gradual empowerment of the religious elite and the bureaucratization of Shariah laws independent of any democratic discussion to the detriment of an open-minded civil society in Malaysia. He then proceeds to an important discussion of the conundrums of Shariah implementation or "syariazation" in Malaysia, with particular attention given to its negative impact on traditional Malay culture, marriage and also towards non-Muslim affairs. He concludes with a valuable discussion of how Christians can respond practically to the increased role of Shariah in state and society.

In the conclusion to this volume, John Cheong draws out key themes from the various papers and offers a set of helpful reflections on how churches that live under varying degrees of Shariah law can respond to the pressures that inevitably arise in such contexts.

Readers will see that this volume is designed to address several goals. First, it tracks the process of how Shariah expands in a number of different national and regional contexts. Second, it pays particular attention to the Muslim-majority countries of Southeast Asia, where expanding Shariah is very much a part of the early twenty-first century. Third, it aims for a pragmatic function, to equip Christians to survive and flourish in societies where Shariah has an increasing sway. With the insight of comparing how it expands differently based on particular socio-cultural and political contexts and how it is variously implemented, it is hoped that the Church will be thus equipped for its future under the shadow of Shariah.

References

Effendy, B. 2003. *Islam and the State in Indonesia*, Singapore: ISEAS.

Hefner, Robert W. ed. 2011. *Shari'a politics: Islamic law and society in the modern world*. Bloomington, IN: Indiana University Press.

Jamhari, 2003. "Mapping Radical Islam in Indonesia", *Studia Islamika* 10/3.

Maghniyyah, M.J. 1995. *The Five Schools of Islamic Law: Al-Hanafi, al-Hanbali, al-Ja'fari, al-Maliki, al-Shafi'i*, Qum, Iran: Ansariyan, 383.

al-Misri, Ahmad ibn Naqib. 1994. *Reliance of the Traveller: A Classic Manual of Islam Sacred Law*, trans. and ed. Nuh Ha Mim Keller, Beltsville, Maryland: Amana.

"Muslims against Sharia", http://muslimsagainstsharia.blogspot.com/, viewed 11 July 2017.

Rashid, A. 2010. *Taliban: Militant Islam, Oil & Fundamentalism in Central Asia*, 2nd ed., New York: I. B. Tauris.

Schacht, J. 1974. "Islamic Religous Law," in *The Legacy of Islam*, 2nd ed., ed. Joseph Schacht and C. E. Bosworth, Oxford: Oxford University Press, pp.392–403.

"Shari'a: Inequality and Excessiveness", *Kairos Journal*, http://www.kairosjournal.org, viewed 11 July 2017.

Sloane-White, P. 2017. *Corporate Islam: Sharia and the modern workplace*. New York: Cambridge University Press.

Solomon, S. and Wakeling, K. 2009. *A Comparison Table of Shari'ah Law and English Law*, London: Christian Concern for our Nation.

Part A

Shariah's Origins and Unfolding in the World

Reflections on the meaning of Sharī'a

Dr Olaf Schumann

Preliminary remarks[1]

What is called *"sharī'a"* is not "law" in the classical sense but a set of guidelines for Muslims to arrange their daily lives according to the precepts of God. This understanding fits also with the original use of the term, which meant "the path to a well of living water", signifying a path to a spring of life in the desert. In Religion the spring of life is the Word of God. According to the scholars (*'ulamā'*), it is rooted in the revelation (*waḥy*), and the only revelation accepted in Islam as genuine and undisputed is the Qur'an.

Nowadays the Qur'an is commonly called the "Sacred Qur'an", or the "Holy Qur'an". But this expression only appears in Western languages, where it is used to challenge the Christian understanding of the "Holy Bible". However, this expression rarely occurs in languages traditionally used by the Muslims. In Arabic, expressions such as *"al-Qur'ān al-qudūs"*, or *"al-Qur'ān al-muqaddas"* do not occur. It is, or at least it was, rendered as *"al-Qur'ān al-karīm"*, the "Noble Qur'an". *"Qudūs"* (Holy) and its derivations are only to be used with regard to God and His **spoken** word.

The Qur'an as a written or printed book is mixed with human activity, and it can even be touched by "unclean" hands – though Muslims may try to prevent non-Muslims from touching it. It is also usually stored in the highest shelf of a bookshelf. A Muslim student of mine once protested when his neighbour in the class laid his Bible, together with other books, on the floor, declaring "That is not a proper place for Holy Scripture". There is only one man-made

---

[1] Cf. also my articles "Hukum Sharī'a dan Pemisahan Agama dengan Negara", in: J. Mardimin, *Mempercakapkan Relasi Agama & Negara*. Jogjakarta: Pustaka Pelajar 2011, 76-106; "Social and Political Law and Ethics in Islam", in: Michael Press (ed.), *Introduction to Lutheran Ethics*. Kota Kinabalu: STS-Lutheran Study Centre 2014, p. 190-220.

location where the root "*q-d-s*" is used, and that is "*al-bait al-maqdis*", or "*al-Quds*", namely Jerusalem. This is influenced by the older Jewish (Hebrew) tradition, where Jerusalem was (and is) called "*bēt ha-miqdash*". Interestingly, even the Ka'ba in Mecca is not "*qudūs*", but "*sharīf*", exalted or mostly honoured.

The same exclusive use also applies to some other terms, like "divine"; it becomes a matter of controversy with regard to *sharī'a* when it is called the "divine Law". There is nothing divine except God, and the term "*sharī'a ilāhiyya*" is not found in any Arabic writing. Again, in Western languages "divine Law" may be used, but the authoritative language for Islam is Arabic, not English. Modern Malay/Indonesian often seems to follow English semantic rules more closely than the original Arabic ones, in contrast to classical Malay. This makes it easier to be understood by English-speaking people including Muslims, but sometimes understanding the original intention and religious sensitivity can be distorted through this process. Some Muslims sense a smell of *shirk* (idolatrous association) behind such imported use. The teachings of *tauḥīd* are very strict in this respect: *tauḥīd* not only means "unity" in a dogmatic sense, but refers to the act of "confessing the Unity", pointing to the important role of the confessor himself.

Sharī'a is widely believed by Muslims to be revealed by God.[2] How does "the" revelation (in Islam), i.e. the Qur'an, correspond to this claim?

Sharī'a in the Qur'an and Hadith

In the whole text of the Qur'an, which contains more than 6000 verses, the term *sharī'a* is mentioned one time, and other words derived from the same verbal root (*sh-r-'* / ش ر ع) four times, namely, *shir'a* (almost synonymous with *sharī'a*) (once), as a verb (twice), and as *shurra'an* (once). In order to clarify the contextual meaning of these words, they are presented in order:[3]

شرع لكم من الدين ما وصى به نوحا والذي أوحينا إليك وما وصّينا به إبرهيم وموسى وعيسى أن أقيموا الدين ولا تتفرّقوا فيه

الشورى {٤٢} ١٣

---

[2] *The World's Muslims: Religion, Politics and Society*, Washington, D.C.: Pew Research Center, 2013, 41.

[3] I follow the Arabic text and English translation of *The Holy Qur'ân*, ed. by King Fahd Holy Qur'ān Printing Complex, al-Madinah al-munawwarah 1410 AH.

> The same religion has He established for you (*shara'a lakum*) as that which He enjoined on Noah – that which we have sent by inspiration to thee – and which we enjoined on Abraham, Moses, and Jesus: namely, that ye should remain steadfast in Religion and make no divisions therein (Q42: 13).

Also on another occasion the Qur'an uses it as a verb:

أم لهم شركؤا شرعوا لهم من الدين ما لم يأذن به الله ولولا كلمة الفصل لقضى بينهم وإن الظالمين لهم عذاب أليم

الشورى ﴿٤٢﴾ ٢١

> What! Have they partners who have established for them some Religion (*shara'ū lahum min ad-dīn*) without the permission of Allah? Had it not been for the decree of Judgement, the matter would have been decided between them. But verily the wrong-doers will have a grievous Chastisement (Q 42:21).

The meaning is somewhat unclear in the following passage, which mentions a people living close to the sea and having a special experience on the Sabbath:

إذ يعدون في السَّبت إذ تأتيهم حيتانهم يوم سبتهم شرَّعا ويوم لا يسبتون لا تأتيهم

الأعراف ﴿٧﴾ ١٦٣

> Behold they transgressed in the matter of the Sabbath. For on the day of their Sabbath their fish did come to them, openly (holding up their heads).[4] But on the day they had no Sabbath, they came not (Q 7:163).

The word *shir'a* is closely related to *sharī'a*. It appears once in the Qur'an when the relationship between the different religions are discussed:

وأنزلنا إليك الكتاب بالحق مصدِّقا لما بين يديه من الكتاب ومهيمنا عليه فاحكم بينهم بما أنزل الله ولا تتبع أهواءهم عمَّا جآءك من الحق لكل جعلنا منكم شرعة ومنهاجا ولو شآء الله لجعلكم أمة واحدة

المائدة ﴿٥﴾ ٤٨

> To thee We sent the Scripture in truth confirming the Scripture that came before it, and guarding it in safety; so judge between them by what Allah hath revealed, and follow not their vain desires, diverging from the truth that has come

---

[4] Or alternatively, "in long rows".

to Thee. To each among you have We prescribed a Law[5] and an Open Way. If Allah had so willed He would have made you a single people (Q 5: 48)

About *sharī'a* the Qur'an states:

ثم جعلناك على شريعة من الأمر فاتبعها لا تتبع أهواء الذين لا يعلمون

الجاثية ﴿٤٥﴾ ١٨

Then we put thee on the right Way of Religion: so follow Thou that (Way), And follow not the desires of those who know not (Q45: 18).

When *sh-r-'* is used as a verb, translators in Medina usually render it as "to establish". The two nouns *sharī'a* and *shir'a* basically mean "a way", particularly a way to a water well, which may also be termed as *sharī'a* pointing to its life-giving power. Metaphorically this meaning has been transferred to the Qur'an which is also the source of (eternal) Life, a well-known metaphor in the traditions of the monotheistic religions.

It would be useful to consider briefly the second authoritative source of Islamic thought, the Hadith. The *Encyclopedia of Islam* gives a short account of the use of *sharī'a* and related terms in this branch of Islamic sciences, based on the findings of Arend Wensinck which were published in his voluminous *Concordance* to the Hadith. For the term in its singular form, there is only one reference: "the community shall remain in the *sharī'a*," and it is clear from the context that again "the path" is meant. For its plural form (*sharā'i'*) there are 12 references mentioned, mostly in locutions like *sharā'i' al-Islam* or *sharā'i' al-īmān,* "rules of Islam" or "rules of Faith". It may be interesting for Christians to note that in Christian theological terminology, the term *sharī'at al-īmān* could also be used for the Creed, or the *"regula fidei"*; the Nestorian convert Ali at-Tabari (10th century) used the term also for his "Islamic Creed" which he formulated in analogy to the Christian Creed.[6] This means that in these early times, *sharī'a* and its cognates were more understood as theological expressions than those of law. The verbal form *shara'a* only occurs once in the Hadith: "God has laid down for his prophet the rules of guidance" (*shara'a li-nabī-hi*

---

[5] As a parallel to *minhāj* ("open Way") the translation of *shir'a* as "Law" seems to be somewhat pretentious. See also the next quotation.

[6] Olaf Schumann, *Jesus the Messiah in Muslim Thought.* Delhi-Hyderabad: ISPCK/Henry Martyn Institute 2002.

sunan al-hudā).[7] Again it is linked to 'guidance' but makes no allusion to 'law'. As is indicated by the last quotation from the Hadith, what had been 'established' by God became the 'habit' (*sunna*)[8] or rule for guiding His people. Therefore, *sharī'a* in the earlier stages of the development of Islamic thought may also be translated as 'guideline', fitting with its original meaning as the direction to be followed to the wells of Life.

Sharī'a and Revelation

Sharī'a is often said to be revealed by God, as stated earlier. There is no hint at all in the whole of the Qur'anic corpus that *sharī'a* was understood either in the Qur'an or by Muhammad himself as a compilation of rules and prescriptions written down and demanded to be obeyed in a literal sense. It may be said – and we can accept – that the *sharī'a* **has its roots** in the Qur'an. But in this metaphor the roots are different from the trunk, and again different from the branches and leaves. They are related and interdependent, but they are not identical. And when studying the *sharī'a* as it is understood and practiced nowadays, even its identity with the roots may often be questioned.

This problem is, however, inherent from the beginning. The "roots" were understood as being guidelines, or the "way" in the original sense of the term. But the details, or branches (*furū'* in the terminology of *ilm al-fiqh*), were compiled by the *'ulamā'*, and collected either from the Qur'an or other accepted sources, or *uṣūl*. In short, the compilation of the *sharī'a* is not the work of God or the angel Jibril as the transmitter of the revelation; it is also not the work of Muhammad – if it were, then the hadith should be more vocal about this matter – but entirely the result of human efforts; *'ulamā'* are prone to error as are other humans.

The fact that in the early times of Islam, the *sharī'a* was **not** understood as a compilation of rules or laws is quite clear in the terminology used in the science of Islamic Law, namely the *'ilm al-fiqh*. *Sharī'a* was handled by the *'ulamā'* or the scholars, but they had no executive power, although they often tried to get it (in continuous strife between the *'ulamā'* and the *umarā'* [plural of *amīr*, ruler]). A *modus vivendi* was found: the rulers were relatively free in deciding the laws (Malay: *undang-undang*) of the country, and these

---

[7] Cf. the above quotation from Q42:13.

[8] "*Sunnan*" in the quotation is the plural form of "*sunna*", habit.

were the *qawānīn* (singular: *qānūn*). They should not contradict principles or rules laid down in the *sharī'a*, but they should be practicable for ruling the kingdom. But, of course, the rulers usually had different understandings of morals and human virtues from the scholars. Therefore, the *qawānīn* may be considered to represent "secular" law from the beginning, appearing religious on the surface but in content being oriented towards the pragmatic needs of the kingdom. Only weak rulers compromised with the *'ulamā'*; strong rulers made their points.

This is also expressed in the *Undang-undang Melaka* (the Laws of Malacca),[9] to mention just one example of literature from the Southeast Asian region. One of the first tasks of a new ruler is said to fix the *undang-undang* (legal codes) in his kingdom.[10] Also important for our discussion is the understanding that even in this context, the *sharī'a* is understood as a guideline and point of orientation, but not a codex of explicit laws and prescriptions. The *sharī'a* is, or should be, dynamic, applicable in various situations and under different conditions. It should correspond to the Qur'anic statements that it is established by God. Any authority that tries to make it an eternal set of defined rules and prescriptions contradicts not only the Qur'an but also the history of *sharī'a* in the Islamic world, where a unified corpus of *sharī'a* was never produced – which would have been produced had it been divine revelation. As a compilation of the *'ulamā'*, the *sharī'a* is a typical product of the religious dogmatism occurring in almost every religion, demanding absolute obedience and claiming a divine authorization. However, it is in fact also a mixture of divine wisdom and human error. Human error becomes obvious when one of the basic axioms of the Qur'an is neglected: that God does not burden any of His creatures with something which it cannot bear. To respect this axiom was usually considered to be the very humane side of God's instructions. Many of the rules and prescriptions imposed in *sharī'a* nowadays contradict not only the Qur'an but also the traditional principles of *sharī'a*.

---

[9] "Undang-Undang Melaka", https://en.wikipedia.org/wiki/Undang-Undang_Melaka, accessed 9 May 2017.

[10] Liaw Yock Fang, *Undang-undang Melaka*. The Hague 1976, p. 62 (Malay) or p. 63 (English).

Early developments of the meaning of sharī'a

The influence of Jewish (and Christian) thinking about the Torah should not be understated. The original meaning of "Torah" was not "law" but guidance. This meaning did not completely disappear, although in the time of Jesus, the tendency to legalize the Torah and make it a corpus of definite prescriptions and laws was obvious, a tendency which increased when Islamic thinking experienced its formative period and, either incidentally or not, in the wake of compiling the Talmud at the same time. Both Jews and Christians started to use Arabic also in their doctrinal deliberations. In the 10th century, the Jewish Bible (Old Testament) was translated into Arabic in Egypt. It is interesting that the term "Torah" was not usually rendered as *taurāt* in Muslim scriptures, but as *sharī'a*. This shows an awareness of the original meaning of both terms. But in Judaism, since approximately the time of Jesus, Torah was understood as being divided into two parts: the written Torah as documented in the Bible, and the oral Torah which was called *Halakha*, derived from the verb *halakh* and meaning also "way". As an aspect of the Torah, it was considered to have its origin also in Moses' teaching, but as oral tradition it was open to the discussions of the scribes which focused on its practical inclinations and also added rules which did not correspond to the original intention of the Torah and, among others, triggered the wrath of Jesus. These discussions of the oral Torah were compiled and became the essential part of the *Mishna*, and as such of the *Talmud*. Essentially, the *Halakha* was understood as an explanation and interpretation of the written Torah. The practical aspects of the *Halakha* also finally had an impact on early Christianity, namely, in the Greek form of *hodos*. Since neither in Hebrew nor in Greek did a word for "religion" exist, the "religion" established by Christ was called the "*hodos tou Christou*", the way of the Messiah, differing from the ways of the Pharisees and scribes.[11] Here again it becomes clear that the emphasis of these terms is not the demand of obedience to law but an invitation to translate God's will as it is taught by the scholars into practical life which, of course, is conducted before the living God, but also taking into account the social and cultural conditions of the environment. The scholars always had to fight with the fact – although they never accepted it as a serious challenge

---

[11] Acts 11:26.

– that there neither did nor does exist a written corpus named *"sharī'a"* obligatory for the whole Islamic community.

In this context, another form of the root *sh-r-'* gained more and more popularity among the Islamic scholars, namely, the term *shar'*. Regarding the meaning of the verb as mentioned above with God as the subject, *shar'* may now also refer to a system or compilation of rules and laws issued by God. As such, *shar'* may also be used in line with *waḥy*, revelation, stressing the moral obligation of the believers to obey the will of God as communicated through His revelation. Thus *shar'* can mean "revelation" with an emphasis on verses with a legal intention. Since the prophet is the main communicator of the revelation, he may now also be called the *shāri'*, 'the one who gives the revealed guidelines'. Later on, this title was also used to refer to the jurists in the sense that they compiled these guidelines.

Sharī'a and Dīn (religion)

In Islamic theology (*Kalām*), the meaning of the different cognates tends to culminate in one, in *sharī'a*; the first phrase in Q42: 13 links the root with *dīn*, religion. This verse evokes the impression that *dīn* is revealed, and therefore cannot be contradictory in itself. But at the same time, the followers of the different prophets, who transmitted the same *dīn*, seem to make distinctions between their rules, and thus a plurality enters into the concept of Oneness: it becomes more restricted to *dīn* being One only, whereas the *sharā'i'* (plural) among them differ. Whatever the reason for this may be, the prophet Muhammad and his followers are advised to maintain those *sharā'i'* which they find in what has been "established" for them. To implement the *sharā'i'* of the others is their own affair and responsibility.

At this point we could consider an interesting derivation from the former terminology which can mislead people unaccustomed to a properly defined use of different terms. As stated above, the religion (*dīn*) must remain one, while the *sharī'a* may differ. This sounds similar – but is not more than similar – to a Qur'anic expression appearing in almost identical form in the "Treaty of Medina"[12] which united the Muslims in Yathrib under the spiritual leadership

---

[12] Alfred Guillaume, *The Life of Muhammad, a translation of Ibn Ishaq's Sirat Rasul Allah*, Karachi Oxford University Press, 21st impression, 2007, 231-33.

of Muhammad[13] but at the same time separated them from the Jews who also lived in Yathrib.[14] In paragraph 25 of that treaty two dimensions of religious life are mentioned and at the same time are separated clearly:

Ummat͞u 'llah ummat͞un wāhida: the **people** of God is one.

But then there follows:

Li-l-muslimīna dīnuhum, wa-li-l-Yahūd dīnuhum:

For the Muslims **their religion** (*dīn*)[15], and for the Jews **their religion**.

The significance is as follows. The community, or people of God, namely those who worship the One God, form also only one community, umma, although the *sharā'i'* which they follow in their worship may be different. As "religious" communities they are different because they follow different prophets as founders of the respective community, or *dīn*.[16] In certain matters – e.g. in matters of food, but also in religious rituals etc. – the directives (*sharā'i'*) of God to them differed. Therefore it should not happen that the adherents of one prophet try to force the adherents of another prophet to leave their community and follow that of their prophet. There is no need of conformity among the different religious communities; they may differ but they should not view each other with hatred or contempt. Logically, these attitudes have no place in a prophetic religion, because as believers they are members of one *umma*, venerating the One God albeit in different ways.

These remarks show that there has been a shift with regard to those aspects which demand unity, and those which allow differences. While in the "Treaty of Medina" the guidelines of a community are closely linked to the understanding of *dīn* and allow diversity, a remarkable change took place in the later developments of Islamic thought.

---

[13] Which therefore later was named *Madīnat an-nabī* (the city of the Prophet).

[14] There were no Christian settlers in that oasis at that time.

[15] The meaning of *dīn* actually is not only "religion" but a "religious community".

[16] It must be remembered that *dīn* does not only mean "religion" but basically a community which adheres to a religion. - The dispute whether *dīn* is one only or appears as a plurality arose later when interpreting Q3: 19: Verily, the religion with God is *islām*. Does "*islām*" point to the formal religion, "Islam", or is the generic meaning implied: "surrender to God"? Maybe one result of this dispute was the later use of *milla* for the non-Islamic religions. In the above mentioned Sura 5: 48 even a plurality of the umma is mentioned.

The mutual estrangement caused a growing tendency to exclusiveness. Terms like *umma* and *dīn* were focused more and more on the Islamic community only, employing for the Christian and Jewish communities more and more their own terms which originated in the Aramaic language: *milla*, instead of *dīn*, with the *umma* as *ummatu 'llāh* confined to the Muslims.

The term *sharī'a* followed this development under two aspects, like the other terms: according to the jurists, the Islamic *sharī'a* is relevant only for those who are members of the Islamic *dīn*. For those who are not members of it but follow another *milla*, the *sharī'a* of their *dīn* is binding, and they have to arrange themselves according to how they want to implement it. Even in the traditional caliphates a strict separation in matters of (religious) law was observed. This was, of course, easier in kingdoms in which the concept of citizens and their equality before the law of a "state" (a state for all citizens without difference) was unknown. A diversity of groups among the subjects makes it easier to deal also with a diversity of laws. And this is, of course, contradictory to any modern understanding of a "state", the sovereignty of which is identified with its sovereignty on the law used in its territory. This plurality can only be practiced in a *"daula"*, which means a monarchy which is based on the sovereignty of the ruler or his family. For a *Negara* (in Malay: state) which is based on the sovereignty of the people it does not fit.

We will now turn to another crucial question which is not a subject of controversy in Islamic circles alone: the relationship between *sharī'a*, or "religious law" in general, and the ruling power and its law. Is there a separation between the two, or between *dīn* and reign similar to the separation between *regnum* and *sacerdotium* in traditional Christian kingdoms (or, as some like to phrase it, between *dīn wa-daula*)[17]? Usually it is claimed that such a separation would be contradictory to Islamic fundamentals.

Religious and Worldly Affairs in Law

A common question relates to the position the prophet Muhammad had in Madina. Was he a ruler? A widely held contemporary view is that firstly, he was the leader of the Meccan migrants (*al-*

---

[17] *Daula* means "*dynasty*". To translate it by "*negara*", or "*state*", is extremely misleading and causes much confusion among Muslim intellectuals when comparing it with Western concepts.

muhājirūna) who moved with him to Yathrib, later called Madina. When they were accepted as equal citizens, he became a member of the *shūrā*, the consulting and governing body of the community in which the leaders of the other tribes or groups were also present. As the prophet, he was highly respected and enjoyed a special position. But he was still not in a position of sole leadership. In voting his advice could also be rejected. His special and unique position, however, was, as repeatedly stressed in the "Treaty of Madina", his (continuing) role as a mediator (*wasit*). That was, as may be remembered, the function for which he was invited to come to Yathrib. According to ancient Arab traditional law, two fighting parties who were not able to settle their conflict among themselves might invite a neutral mediator to settle their dispute, and then both parties had to accept his decision. Now, again according to the "Treaty", God stood behind him and secured the correctness of his decisions. Since Muhammad's advice and judgments were regarded as wise and well balanced, this role added decisively to the respect and affection he enjoyed in Yathrib/Madina. But formally speaking, he was neither a president nor a monarch. His role does not support any claim raised nowadays of the claimed strong relationship between religion and state, and that the use of *sharī'a* is legitimated by Muhammad's role in Madina. He was, to use the Latin phrase, *primus inter pares*, the first among equals. Even in legal matters he only gave advice but never promulgated laws, and these were actually linked to cases brought before him. He indicated the guidelines, stressed the principles and invited others to accept them, but he never demanded unconditioned obedience, and moreover tended to give advice in favour of the culprit. The literature of the Hadith presents a multitude of examples, and the present-day practitioners of *sharī'a* should be aware of that; unfortunately they seldom are.

On one particular point, the political construction of Madina was progressive for its day. The *shūrā* assembled the leaders of the different tribes who were respected and supported and usually also appointed by the members of their tribes, and they were the practical governing body of the community.[18] In the words of Mahmūd Shaltūt, former Grand Shaikh of al-Azhar in Cairo from 1958-63: "The *shūrā* is the basis for the administration of public

---

[18] Mahmūd Shaltūt underlined the meaning of *shūrā* for the life of the umma: M. Syaltūt, *Al-Islām: 'Aqīda wa-Sharī'a*. al-Qāhira: Dār al-Qalam, 3rd ed. n.y. (ca. 1965) pp. 458 ff. Shaltūt particularly points to Q42 "*Al-Syūrā*".

affairs".[19] Through its members, the voice of the people was present, also in decision making. Since Muhammad was not a sole ruler or monarch, he did not appoint or indicate a successor to continue his activities after his death. He left the decision about his successor to the *shūrā* responsible to the *umma* as a whole, and thus the "*khalīfat an-nabī*" (successor of the prophet) **was elected** by the *umma*. This procedure was maintained for four occasions, and in Islamic historiography this period is praised as the golden age of Islam, the time of the four rightly guided caliphs. Their legitimacy was rooted in the *umma*. This changed with the fifth caliph, Mu'awiya, the founder of the dynasty of the Umayyads. Because of a lack of public support, Mu'awiya proclaimed himself as successor to the fourth caliph, Ali, after Ali's assassination. Since Mu'awiya had no legitimacy from the *umma*, he claimed that he got his legitimacy directly from God. Thus the foundation was laid for the later claim of Muslim rulers that they are *khalīfatu 'llāh*, legitimized by God, and not by the *umma* or the *shūrā* as its representative, as had been the case in the beginning. And, moreover, he also decreed (in 672 CE) that his son Yazid should become his successor after his death. But what happened under Mu'awiya was described by the later Muslim historians as abandoning the roots of Islam. The Golden Age of the *khulafā ar-rāshidūn*, i.e. the first four rightly guided caliphs, had come to its end. The caliph, through his personal attire and the wisdom of his rule should give a good example and led his subjects on the way of truth. If he were unable to do this and instead of it led his subjects astray – thus endangering their access to eternal salvation – then he should be replaced. Among scholars who were not linked to the court, and particularly among the Muslim philosophers, the opinion prevailed that the leadership of the caliph was a political and not a religious one. He must not be a theologian, and the "religious" aspect of his leadership was focused on his *taqwā*, or piety and obedience to the precepts of the religion; but to formulate them was the task of the *'ulamā'*. This opinion prevailed until the end of the caliphate in 1924, when the last caliph, invested by the republican Turkish parliament in 1922 but stripped of all his political functions, was dismissed and the caliphate terminated. But many caliphs and their obedient *'ulamā'* did not subscribe to that conviction. Already the third caliph, Uthman, the uncle of Mu'awiya, refused to step down after he had lost credibility. For that he was murdered. Later on the

---

[19] كانت الشورى اصلا في إدارة الشئون الجماعية, *ibid*. p. 460.

position of the rulers was sanctioned by the slogan *Islām dīn wa-daula* (Islam is religion and monarchy).[20] Not the *shūrā* nor the *umma*, but the ruler himself (or God) legitimized his rule, supported by some *'ulamā'* and jurists.

This position was further strengthened when the last Ottoman caliphs met with increasing opposition because of their growing religious ambitions. But the practical distinction (and later on also the separation between religious law and "secular" or dynastical/political law) had spread very early into the domain of Islamic Jurisprudence (*fiqh*). It developed mainly in two branches: (a) the *'ibādāt* (matters concerning religious rites and ceremonies and their practice), and (b) the *mu'āmalāt* (matters concerning social and political issues).[21] Both branches of the *fiqh*, *'ibādāt* and *mu'āmalāt* were strictly separated, and this was also obvious in the main and basic difference which also decided about the methods used in both branches of *fiqh*. The rites (*'ibādāt*) have a tendency to be conservative; they can survive for a long time without many changes, because of God's supposed immutability; therefore the worship of Him does not require much adaptation to changing situations or conditions on the human side. This is different from the *mu'āmalāt*, which demand continuous change and adaptation to the continuously changing social and political situations. *Mu'āmalāt* must be dynamic, while *'ibādāt* tend to be static.

Sharī'a, as a practical guideline to live in harmony with God's will and expect with joy the future with Him is not directly linked to *Fiqh* as a religious science. But it has a great affinity to *'ibādāt* although it is much more exposed to social changes than the *'ibādāt* are. But that insight seems to have not yet reached a number of present day *'ulamā'* who also turn to an imagined past in order to design the future. Very much in contradiction to the Qur'anic and classical understandings of the *sharī'a* is its use as a camouflaged penal code, in order to protect it against any criticism. Ideas and practices are petrified and sanctified which have long since lost any relevance for or impact on dynamic societies, and it is not by accident that in the course of Islamic history, the use of *sharī'a* became more and more restricted to personal, family or communal

---

[20] The usual translation "Islam is Religion and State" is not correct: *daula* means monarchy or dynasty, not state.

[21] It is noteworthy that the *'Ibādāt* are part of the Jurisprudence (*Fiqh*), while Theology (*'Ilm al-Kalām*) forms a separate branch of the Sciences of Islam.

affairs. But nowadays, even practicing the "*ḥudūd*" (severe punishment of certain crimes) is declared to be "*wājib*"(obligatory). To this distortion, the Sudanese world-renowned scholar Abdullahi an-Na'im said during a visit to Kuala Lumpur: "Describing these crimes as hudud crimes is the way of jurists, it is not in the Qur'an, it is not in the Sunnah".[22]

This shift in understanding and applying the *sharī'a* nowadays has deeper roots. In recent times, a shift in applying the different methods used in classical *fiqh* became apparent. It seems that nowadays the *mu'āmalāt* are more and more treated by those "jurists" like the *'ibādāt* as being unchangeable in eternity, viewing any changes with great suspicion or even as *bid'a*t (heresy) and taking an imagined past as point of orientation. Of course, this past is presented as the golden age of prophet Muhammad and his companions who, in traditional terminology, where called the *salaf*. But this imagined golden past has little to do with the reality of that past during Muhammad's lifetime as far as it can be reconstructed. By abandoning basic methods and principles while promulgating their *sharā'i'* these present day "jurists" dissociated themselves from the historic *salaf* and their ideals. It seems more evident that a projection of the past is produced with the intention to replace the facts of that past by imaginations which fit more to the actual desires than to historic reality. Not progress but regress is the result, and this stagnation has its effect on all aspects of social life, the religious one included, as we have mentioned. It was the critique against *taqlīd* (imitation) of traditions and rules rooted in either the real or an imagined past which was the focus of the former reformers of Islamic thought, making it responsible for the backwardness of Islamic societies. This focus seems to have vanished. Moreover, by interfering with the internal affairs of other religious communities and applying the "Islamic" *sharī'a* – as they interpret it – to non-Muslims as well, essential rules of the social order established by Muhammad and his contemporaries, the *salaf*, are revoked. One aspect of religious life which suffers greatly under this perversion is the desire of devout Muslims to practise sober religious principles and convictions in social, public life, particularly in plural societies. This can be practiced properly when guided by a *sharī'a* which is illuminated by the beauty and wisdom of God, and not decreed by the brutal fancies of misguided scholars or rulers.

---

[22] Quoted by *Daily Express* (Sabah), June 3, 2016, p. 17 from an interview given in Kuala Lumpur.

From Shariah to Society: Case Studies from Egypt, Pakistan and Indonesia

Prof Peter G Riddell

Islam has been in resurgence across the world since the 1970s (Berger & Sonneveld 2010, p. 65; Carvalho 2009, p. 4). This raises a key question: resurgence from what? A survey of Islam since its inception in the early seventh century points to a cyclical pattern in its historical trajectory.

The cycle can be divided into three macro phases. The first phase includes the articulation of the theory and principles of Islam. This phase is represented by Muhammad's ministry in Mecca and Medina (610-32), as well as the immediately following centuries where Islamic scholars and jurists shaped the emerging faith.

The second phase is reflected in the diverse manifestations of Islam as lived by its adherents. This involves a movement away from a notion of centralised orthodoxy to a kaleidoscopic diversity, whether based on sectarian differences, mystical reflections, syncretistic expressions drawing on pre-Islamic faiths, ethnic and cultural factors, and so forth.

The third phase typically follows periods of Islamic decline. It involves a recognition of that decline, usually attributed to Muslims drifting away from the true faith, and a dramatic call for reform. This is the phase of resurgence. The reformist call is directed towards a return to the original models and principles articulated in the first phase. Typically, it involves a call for Shariah law, based on the view that following the example of Muhammad will lead to Islamic greatness once again.

While this three-phase cycle applies at the macro level of broad Islamic history, it can also be applied to individual Islamic states and societies, with different states being at different points on the cycle; while some are comfortably immersed in diverse expressions of the faith, others are in resurgence, seeking to get back to the basics, as it were.

The present paper considers more closely a key element of the call for reform in the phase of resurgence; namely, the call for the implementation of Shariah law. We will focus on three case studies: Egypt, Pakistan, and the Indonesian province of Aceh. The history of these three majority Islamic societies suggests that they followed a similar trajectory along the Shariah path that, for convenience sake, could be seen in eight stages.

Stage 1: Narratives of a glorious past lost

In Egypt, Pakistan and Aceh the foundations of the increasing clamour for the implementation of Shariah law in recent decades lie in a perception by Muslim activists of a glorious Islamic past that had been lost.

In the case of Egypt, the Islamic conquest in 641 AD ushered in a period of Islamic greatness under successive dynasties. In its earliest years, Islamic Egypt was constituted by a pre-Islamic population under the control of Islamic garrisons. But as the centuries passed, the population became increasingly Islamised, enjoying the benefits of different dynasties: the Abbasids, the Fatimids, the Mamluks and the Ottomans. Although historical records suggest that in fact the Ottomans were regarded as foreign conquerors by many Egyptians in the period that Egypt was an *eyalet* (administrative province) of the Ottoman Empire (1517-1867), today's nostalgic Shariah activists look back to a period of perceived Islamic dominance and greatness across these dynasties.

A common refrain among Shariah activists is that the glories of Islamic Egypt were stolen by non-Islamic foreign powers, with the key usurpers being European colonizers. Between 1798 – 1801 Egypt was invaded by France under Napoleon's leadership, during which time the French caused permanent offence by stabling their cavalry in the mosque of Al-Azhar (Browne 1907, p. 170). During the period of French presence, Niqula al-Turk, court poet to Bashir Shihab II, the Maronite ruler of Lebanon, visited Cairo and noted that the French had erected a monument, which they termed 'the tree of freedom'. However, Al-Turk noted that local Egyptians referred to it as 'the sign of the stake that impaled us in the occupation of our kingdom' (Ruthven 2017, p. 1R).

Ever watchful of expanding French power and influence under Napoleon's leadership, the British defeated the French decisively in the Battle of the Nile in August 1798, and combined with the Turks in subsequent years to evict the French from Egypt. Egypt was then ruled by the dynasty of the Ottoman Albanian commander Muhammad Ali (r. 1805-49) and his successors, with its status changing from *eyelet* to *khedivate* (autonomous vassal state) in 1867 during the reign of Isma'il Pasha (r. 1863-79). The British presence became increasingly overt with the opening of the Suez Canal in 1869, and in 1881 they invaded and occupied Egypt, remaining the principal powerbroker in the land for the next forty years.

During the nineteenth century, the role of the traditional *ulama* in political and economic life was gradually eroded by the rise of a professional elite of doctors, teachers and engineers (Fahmy 1998, p. 164) and, as a result, they focused their energies on Islamic educational networks, especially centred on Al-Azhar University and Mosque (Green 1980, p. 41ff). Around the turn of the twentieth century, the lectures of the Grand Mufti of Al-Azhar, Muhammad Abduh, stimulated an awakening of Islamic activism in response to Islam's perceived decline under European colonial control. This represented an important first stage on the journey towards the resurgence that we are witnessing in the modern day.[1]

In the case of Pakistan, the great Mughal Empire (1526-1857) had represented the heyday for Islam in India. Descended from the Mongols who had cut a destructive path across Asia and the Middle East in the thirteenth century, the Mughal emperors succeeded in carving out vast domains for Islam in the subcontinent. Like Egypt, there is clearly a narrative of a glorious Islamic past in Pakistan.

There are similarly good grounds for Muslim activists to consider that the past glories of the Mughal Empire were stolen. The power of the Mughals was gradually eroded with the increasing influence of the British East India Company for 250 years from 1600 (Keay 2010). The company used its own private armies to rule large areas of India. The Indian mutiny of 1857, which was 'motivated by a desire to protect Islam and to rid India of infidels' (Lau 2010, p. 381), led to the British Crown taking control of the Indian territories of the British East India Company, ushering in the century of the British Raj. The Mughals were no more; the past greatness of Islam had been usurped by non-Muslim colonial powers.

In the case of the Indonesian province of Aceh, today's Muslims from the region look back with nostalgia to the era of the great Sultanate of Aceh, established in the early sixteenth century and

---

[1] For a detailed study of the British period in Egypt, cf. Mansfield (1972).

which reached its peak of regional power and influence during the seventeenth century. Al-Attas (1988, p. 33) describes Aceh in 1590 as 'the intellectual and spiritual centre of Islam in the Malay world at that time', and under its most successful ruler, Sultan Iskandar Muda (r. 1607-36), Aceh established a great empire in Sumatra and the Malay peninsula.

Acehnese decline during the eighteenth and nineteenth centuries coincided with ever-expanding Dutch colonial presence in the region. A clash between the two was inevitable as the Dutch control moved northwards in Sumatra. In anticipation, the Sultan of Aceh sent a delegation to the Ottoman court in 1868 to request protection from an impending Dutch attack, seeking to place Aceh under the sovereignty of the Ottomans. In the event, the latter were themselves in decline and were unable to assist.

In 1873 the Dutch attacked the Acehnese capital, quickly capturing the palace of the Sultan, who died soon afterwards. The Dutch announced the annexation of Aceh to the Netherlands East Indies and the end of the war. However, Acehnese resistance continued as guerilla warfare led by religious leaders, the *ulama*, who waged a *jihad* for several decades. The Dutch policy was to attempt to divide and conquer, under the guidance of Snouck Hurgronje, the Advisor on Islamic Affairs to the Dutch colonial government. He recommended that the Dutch crush the ulama and woo the local traditional chiefs, the *uleebalang*. By 1903 much of Aceh had been pacified. In that year Sultan Muhammad Daud Shah, the last Sultan of Aceh (r. 1874-1903), surrendered, and the Dutch abolished the Sultanate.

Stage 2: Foundation of advocacy organisations: nationalist vs Islamist

In the second stage of the Shariah trajectory, organisations were founded for the specific purpose of challenging those powers that had undermined the previously independent Muslim communities. This stage is interesting in that the responses are varied and, while reform is an agreed goal of all involved, the place of Shariah in the reform is contested (Berger & Sonneveld 2010, p. 57).

In Egypt, the British dissolved their protectorate in 1922, providing autonomy for the Egyptian king and parliament. However, they did not relinquish control of all areas, maintaining a key presence in matters of security and defence and consolidating significant influence in matters of trade. Many Egyptians felt that their nation was still far from independent. Furthermore, the future shape of the nation was up for grabs; different organisations emerged, seeking to impose their vision on the nation-formation process.

A key step in this Shariah trajectory occurred in 1928, when Hassan al-Banna founded the Muslim Brotherhood in Ismailia. The platform of this pan-Islamic organisation from the outset was to build a society based upon the Qur'an and the Sunnah, with Shariah law providing the framework of social, legal and political structures. This is expressed in the following terms on the Muslim Brotherhood website:

> At the inception of the group, its founder Imam Al-Banna focused on two main objectives: Liberating the Muslim world from all foreign powers; A free Islamic state to be established in that liberated homeland, based on the tenets and principles of Islam and applies [sic] its social system, and reaches out [sic] to other peoples of the world with the light, mercy, wisdom and guidance of Islam. (*Eighty-Eight Years On, Muslim Brotherhood Stands Steadfast As Ever – for Freedom, Reform*)

With its foundation, the Brotherhood thus set out to promote Shariah, both overtly and subtly, as the Egyptian state took shape during the twentieth century.

The Muslim Brotherhood faced competition in pursuing its goals from other nationalist movements who did not share the vision of building a Shariah state in the new Egypt. Key names in this liberal nationalist movement were Mustafa Kamil (1874-1908) and Saad Zaghlul (1859-1927), the leader of the Wafd movement that sought to unite all Egyptians, Muslim and non-Muslim, in the campaign for independence (Gershoni & Jankowski 1987, p. 43). But what they did share with the Muslim Brotherhood pioneers was a perception that Egypt's glorious past had been stolen by outsiders.

Stage two of the Shariah trajectory is played out similarly in the case of Pakistan. Early nationalist pioneers in British India formed the All-India Muslim League in 1906, designed to serve as a protector of the interests of Indian Muslims. In 1940, the Muslim League, as it came to be known, put its support behind the call for a separate nation for India's Muslims, but theirs was not a call for an independent nation based on Shariah law.

Nevertheless, as in Egypt, the place of Shariah in the longed-for state was a matter of contestation. In 1941, Abul A'la Maududi founded the Jama'at-i Islami, which dedicated its energies to the pursuit of a Shariah-based Islamic state for Muslims as an outcome of the fast-moving Indian independence process. At his inaugural address at the foundation ceremony of the Jama'at, Maududi explained the choice of the organisation's name as representing the goal 'to change the whole system of this world meaning thereby, to change morality, civilization, politics, culture, economics and society. So that [the] God-willed system prevails everywhere' (*Inaugural address by Syed Mawdoodi*, para. 5-6).

Thus, in both Egypt and India, advocacy organisations had been formed that dreamed of regaining past glories, with some committed to implementation of Shariah law in future independent nations, while others were not so committed.

What about the case of Aceh? While the aspirations in that region for Independence from external control were similar, the outcome was somewhat different. Aceh did not, and so far has not, attained independence in its own right. However, with the declaration of independence by the modern nation of Indonesia in 1945, a process was unleashed where activists in Aceh and elsewhere sought to Islamise the new nation.

As the first generation of leaders of the new nation pursued their independence dream, some demanded the inclusion of a statement in the Constitution that guaranteed a role for Shariah Law. This statement became known as the Jakarta Charter (*Piagam Jakarta*) and stipulated an 'obligation for adherents of Islam to practice Islamic law' (Liow 2015, p. 1). The decision to exclude this statement bitterly disappointed Islamist activists, leading to the eruption of the *Negara Islam Indonesia (Darul Islam)* rebellion (1953–1962) against Jakarta rule in several regions of the new nation. The Acehnese branch of the rebellion was led by Teungku Daud Beureueh (1899 – 1987). The rebellion was eventually crushed across the nation by the Indonesian armed forces in 1962 (Sjamsuddin 1985). In Aceh, a negotiated settlement in the late 1950s provided the province with a measure of autonomy in the domains of religious affairs, customary law and education, providing that the implementation of such autonomy did not conflict with the Indonesian Constitution (Effendy 2003, p. 38). This recognition of limited autonomy in Aceh, did not extinguish the desire for independence among many Acehnese. A successor movement to the *Darul Islam* movement was the *Gerakan Aceh Merdeka* (1976-2005), which was established by a former *Darul Islam* leader Hasan di Tiro. The GAM received assistance from outside sources, particularly from Libya, during the 1980s. It was motivated by a range of concerns, not only relating to Shariah aspirations but also including access to the benefits of Aceh's natural resources and discontent with immigration of Indonesians from other regions to Aceh.

While in Egypt and Pakistan, the competition between nationalist and Islamist organisations was clear-cut, in Aceh it took the form of regional Islamist independentism versus nationalist pressure from the central government in Jakarta.

Stage 3: Early Experiment with non-Islamist models of state

The third stage of the Shariah trajectory in our case studies considers the kinds of political structures that were initially adopted in the postcolonial states.

In Egypt, King Farouk, the last in the dynastic line that had begun with Muhammad Ali in 1805, was overthrown in a military coup d'état in 1952. Initially the revolution received the support of the Muslim Brotherhood, who saw it as an opportunity to achieve their goal of an Islamic state based on Shariah law. However, the new Egyptian leader who emerged from the coup, General Gamal Abdel Nasser, was more inclined to socialism than to Shariah. Relations between Nasser's regime and the Muslim Brotherhood deteriorated rapidly. In 1954 the Brotherhood was banned and its headquarters were burned, with thousands of members being arrested.

In this stage of experimentation with non-Islamist models of state, Shariah activism was on the back foot. In 1955 Nasser's regime passed Law 462 to abolish the Shariah courts, and six years later Al-Azhar was placed under the jurisdiction of the Ministry of Endowments by Law 103, which enabled the President to control Al-Azhar appointments, including that of the Grand Shaykh (*Islam and the State under Nasser*).[2] In 1966, the spiritual leader of the Muslim Brotherhood, Sayyid Qutb, was executed. This represented the absolute nadir of Islamist influence and Shariah presence in the new Egyptian nation.

The story in Pakistan was somewhat similar. From the outset of Pakistan's independence in 1947, there was a clear tension between modernist Muslim leaders and those wanting a Shariah-based state (Lau 2010, p. 388). Western parliamentary structures exerted a

---

[2] Cf. also Berger & Sonneveld (2010, p. 60).

strong influence on the father of the nation of Pakistan, Muhammad Ali Jinnah (1876-1948), who was head of the Muslim League from 1913-47 and who had himself spent many years in Britain studying and practising law. He advocated a clear separation between religion and politics (Malik 2008, p. 380) and, in spite of his untimely death in 1948, his influence was clearly stamped on the political structures of Pakistan in this early period (Wolpert 2005).

Jinnah's Muslim League was opposed by two Islam-motivated groupings: Deobandi ultra-conservatives, representing the traditionalist *ulama*, and the Islamist Jama'at-i Islami, led by Sayyid Abul A'la Maududi, who called for the implementation of Shariah and for the barring of non-Muslims from high office in the state. Maududi longed for past idealised Muslim society in India before the British Raj and, beyond that, to the community of the Prophet Muhammad in Medina. Although the momentum lay with the more liberal Muslim League in the early years of Pakistan's independence, Maududi and the Jama'at-i Islami were determined in pushing their own agenda. In 1951 Maududi joined with traditionalists in outlining twenty-two Basic Principles of an Islamic State for presentation to the Constituent Assembly discussing the Constitution of the new nation (Maududi, ch. 6). This led to the framing of the Objective Resolution (resembling the Indonesian Jakarta Charter) which stipulated that 'the Muslims shall be enabled to order their lives in the individual and collective spheres in accordance with the teachings and requirements of Islam' (Shah 2000, p. 247). This ensured that, even in this period of liberal dominance, Islamist priorities remained on the agenda, awaiting the day that the cycle of influence would turn.

Pakistan's first two decades witnessed some enlightened legislation under the influence of progressive political groups. In 1954, a Charter of Women's Rights was passed, and in 1961 the Family Law Ordinance was also passed (*The Muslim Family Laws Ordinance, 1961*), with both bringing a measure of equality for women. The First Constitution (1956) (*The Preamble of the Constitution of Pakistan*) included Section 18 on Fundamental Rights respecting freedom of religion. Nevertheless, some concessions had to be made to more conservative Islamic groups; non-Muslims were prohibited from proselytising among Muslims, while the constitution stipulated that laws must be consistent with Islam.

For Pakistan, the nadir of Islamist influence arrived in 1958, when martial law was declared and a government under General Ayub

Khan took over. His regime was even less inclined to Islamist politics. In the Second Constitution (1962), the word 'Islamic' was dropped from the official name of the state: the 'Islamic Republic of Pakistan' became simply the 'Republic of Pakistan' (*The Republic of Pakistan*), though the original name was restored the following year in a constitutional amendment under pressure from Islamist groups (Lau 2010, p. 393). Moreover, the regime of President Ayub Khan established many reform commissions and committees, with only a few addressing Islamic issues.

With Indonesian independence, Aceh fell under the administrative control of the central Government of Indonesia from Jakarta. Islamism was in retreat under the country's first two presidents. The Sukarno years (1949-66) witnessed the crushing of the Darul Islam movement, as discussed above. The New Order period under President Suharto (1966-1998) was characterized by the marginalization of Islam as a political force across the nation (Riddell, P. 2005, pp. 162-5). In Aceh that process involved the progressive suppressing of the Geurakan Acèh Meurdèka (GAM) in an initial phase (1976-9) and then a more destructive second phase (1989-91) which involved widespread human rights abuses by both sides. Meanwhile, the half century of rule by Sukarno and Suharto saw alternative ideologies predominate: the rise of communist influence under Sukarno, followed by tight military control from Jakarta under Suharto, presented under the semblance of regular elections that were far from being free and fair.

Stage 4: National trauma and crisis

There are many cases in past history where major national trauma has led to a significant restructuring on the political stage. Clear illustrations of this process can be found in our chosen case studies.

Several years prior to the army rebellion in Egypt that brought Nasser to power, the Israeli War of Independence of 1948 had resulted in the victory of Jewish forces over the much more numerous Arab armies arrayed against them. The sense of national humiliation felt in Egypt was a significant factor in the army rebellion which followed. However, in that case, the political transition was from monarchy to a socialist-inspired nationalist regime.

Egypt's relations with the new State of Israel were volatile over the next three decades. In 1956 Egypt was overwhelmed by the combined military forces of Britain, France and Israel, though the resulting occupation of the Sinai peninsula was short-lived owing to American pressure on those three victorious nations to withdraw. A far greater catastrophe from an Egyptian perspective occurred in 1967. In the Six-Day War in June of that year, Israel was victorious against the combined and far more numerous military forces of Egypt, Syria and Jordan, leading to the Israeli occupation of the Sinai Peninsula, the Golan Heights and the West Bank.

The Socialist-inspired nationalist regime of President Nasser was considered by many Egyptians to have failed. This provided exactly the kind of opportunity that the regime's Islamist opponents had been waiting for. The pervasive sense of national trauma was to open the door for the Islamist opposition that had long been calling for a Shariah-based state (Berger & Sonneveld 2010, p. 61).

A somewhat similar train of events took place in Pakistan. Since independence in 1947, the new nations of Pakistan and India had come close to military conflict on many occasions. Indeed, the separation of the two communities in 1947 was a bloody affair, and the two nations fought a short war in 1965 over the disputed territory of Kashmir.

However, 1971 was to bring about the kind of national trauma in Pakistan that Egypt had experienced just four years before. At independence, Pakistan consisted of two parts: West Pakistan and East Pakistan, centred on Bengal. For over twenty years following independence, many East Pakistanis felt that West Pakistan was favoured in the distribution of wealth, power and privilege. An independence movement emerged in East Pakistan, erupting into civil war between the two parts of the nation in 1971. India intervened on the side of the East Pakistan independence movement, leading to the third Indo-Pakistan War. The result was that East Pakistan broke away and declared itself as the independent nation of Bangladesh.

As had occurred in Egypt, this national crisis provided an opportunity for the Islamist opposition to gain support from a humiliated and disenchanted population in the geographically-reduced nation of Pakistan. Islamists claimed Pakistan had fragmented because it had strayed from Islam through its liberal political leadership. This argument struck a chord with many Pakistanis.

In the case of Aceh, the sense of crisis took a different form. After a half century of dominance by two presidents, with Suharto occupying the presidential palace for thirty-two years, the latter figure was forced from power in 1998. This momentous event unleashed a period of dynamic political change and reform, opening up opportunities for Acehnese aspirations that were without precedent in the life of the Indonesian nation.

Stage 5: New leadership that opens the Shariah door

The next stage of the Shariah trajectory consisted of new political leadership that was more open to Shariah-based legislation.

In 1970 President Nasser died and with him died his socialist-inspired model of state. His successor as President was Anwar Sadat, who served in the role from 1970-81. Sadat was in fact not a hardline Islamist. However, he was a pragmatist who was skilled at recognising the winds of change that were blowing through Egypt. He saw that the momentum for change was moving in the direction of Islamist thinking, which represented a fresh paradigm in recent Egyptian political life, at exactly the time that change was needed to overcome the sense of national humiliation resulting from the loss of the Sinai Peninsula to Israel.

This demand for change also derived from social factors. Nasser's socialist system had not solved the widespread problems of poverty and disadvantage in Egypt's rapidly growing population. Because Nasser's state had not been able to satisfactorily address the level of need, religious groups active during this period that were undertaking charitable activities won support in the process. Samuel Tadros describes

> the rise of alternative networks to provide for the needy in the fields of education, health and financial assistance. Inevitably what filled the gap left by the state were religious institutions. Both the church and the rising Islamists witnessed a wide expansion of their activities, ultimately replacing the state in providing for the people. (Tadros 2013a, para. 3)[3]

Tadros' statement indicates that the Church and Islamists were playing a similar role, but they were far from being partners, as Islamists dreamed of a Shariah-based state where non-Muslims would live under Islamic rule. Sadat's courting of the Muslim movements and the latter's resulting empowerment led to interreligious tensions, with clashes erupting between Muslims and Christians in 1972. This led to increasing attempts at government

---

[3] For more comprehensive research by this author, cf. Tadros (2013b).

intervention in the process of appointing Coptic Popes (Ibrahim et al. 1996, pp. 17, 20). The stage was set for rising Christian-Muslim conflict and increased Shariah legislation.

Likewise in Pakistan, national humiliation and trauma led to political change. In 1971 Zulfikar Ali Bhutto of the Pakistan People's Party assumed the presidency, remaining in the position until 1977. Like Sadat in Egypt, Bhutto was no hardline Islamist, but he too could read the winds of change blowing in Pakistan and realised that the dominance of both liberal democratic policies and military rule had been greatly eroded. His period in power opened the door for increased Shariah-based legislation (Lau 2010, pp. 396-7). In turn, his successor as President, General Muhammad Zia-ul-Haq (1978-88) was to ramp up the drive towards a Shariah-based state.

In Indonesia, Suharto's successor as President, Jusuf Habibie (1998-99), triggered a process of democratization that eventually worked in favour of the Acehnese who longed for greater autonomy. Habibie reduced central government troop levels in Aceh as part of a process of devolution, after decades of tightly controlled government from Indonesia's capital. President Habibie's administration also enacted legislation that increased the role of Shariah in the operations of the province of Aceh.

Stage 6: Increasing Shariah-based legislation

Keen to place their stamp on nations that were reeling from a sense of humiliation and trauma, the new leaders of Egypt and Pakistan changed course away from more secularist policies of the past to more Shariah-influenced legislation. Meanwhile, Acehnese provincial leadership was able to use a process of devolution of power to the provinces to raise the Shariah stakes.

In 1971, Egypt's President Sadat, who increasingly termed himself 'the believer President', introduced a new constitution in which Shariah was specified as '*a* principal source of legislation'. In a subsequent constitutional amendment, Islam was declared as the 'religion of state' and Shariah was acknowledged as '*the* principal source of legislation' (Ibrahim et al. 1996, p. 17). [italics mine]

These changes contributed to an increased sense of concern among Egyptian Christians. This concern was heightened in 1977 when a draft law was introduced in the Egyptian Parliament making apostasy from Islam a capital crime, though after Coptic protests, it was withdrawn.

Nevertheless, Sadat's relations with Islamist groups was uneven. Support for him from these groups reached a peak in 1973 after the inconclusive October war in which Egypt attacked Israeli forces in order to wrest control of the Suez Canal and the Sinai peninsula from them. However, Egyptian Islamists were dismayed when Sadat visited Israel and addressed the Israeli parliament, leading to the Egyptian-Israeli Peace Treaty of 1979 even though Sadat later tried to curry favour with his increasingly vocal Islamist opponents. On 14 May 1980 he gave a fiery speech accusing the Coptic Pope of setting up a Christian sub-state in the south of Egypt, concluding his speech with the statement: 'I am a Muslim President of an Islamic country' (Tadros 2013a, para. 17). While it widened the gulf between his regime and Egyptian Christians, it did not bridge the divide with Islamists, who plotted his downfall.

The 1970s in Pakistan witnessed a similar ramping up of Shariah-friendly legislation. In the country's Third Constitution (1973) (*The Constitution of the Islamic Republic of Pakistan*), the Islamic provisions of the first constitution were preserved, and Islam was declared to be 'the state religion'. Non-Muslims were deemed to be ineligible for the post of Prime Minister. The study of Islam was made compulsory in schools. The Red Cross was renamed the Red Crescent in 1974, while Ahmadis were declared to be non-Muslims in the same year.

The pace of change in the direction of Shariah increased noticeably with the coming to power of President Zia-ul Haq, with increasing influence from the Jama'at-i Islami which strongly supported his Islamisation program. A Hudud Ordinance was introduced in 1979, relating to fornication and adultery, with Hudud punishments introduced, including amputation of hands, flogging, and stoning. The following year a Federal Shariah Court was established. In 1984 the Law of Evidence was passed, based on the usual Shariah bias towards Muslim males in court evidence, and in the same year a Law of 'Qisas' and 'Diyat' was put forward, setting the level of compensation/blood money for female victims as half that for males. In one of the most notorious changes in the context of subsequent developments, in 1986 the Pakistan Government inserted Section 295C into the Pakistan Penal Code, specifying life imprisonment or the death penalty for blaspheming the prophet

Muhammad (*Pakistan Penal Code*). The period of blasphemy witch-hunts had begun.

In Indonesia, the period of reform triggered by the fall of President Suharto's regime and the ensuing greater regional autonomy quickly turned into a movement towards Shariah-based legislation in Aceh. On 4 October 1999, Law 44/1999 on 'The Special Status of the Province of Aceh Special Region' was enacted by the Indonesian House of Representatives (DPR) in Jakarta. The designation 'special status' encompassed the right to lead a religious life (the right to introduce 'Syari'at Islam'); the right to implement traditional custom (*adat*); the right to implement education including elements of 'Syari'at Islam'; and the right to involve the religious (Islamic) leadership in policy making (through the creation of a special board of *ulama*) (*Aceh Peace Process Follow-Up Project* 2012, p. 15; Salim 2008, p. 152).

In the wake of Law 44/1999, Aceh witnessed increasing Shariah-related provisions in the legislation of the province. On 19 July 2001, the Indonesian parliament passed Law 18/2001 as the 'Special Autonomy for the Special Region of Aceh', renaming the province Nanggroe Aceh Darussalam (Miller 2006, p. 292). This law guaranteed Aceh seventy percent of its oil and gas revenue, with the remainder going to the central government. The province was also promised eighty percent of total revenue from agriculture and fisheries (Umm Mutma'inna 2002).

The Special Autonomy Law in 2001 led to an initial batch of regulations (*qanun*) (Miller 2006, p. 306ff; Salim 2008, pp. 157-8) such as:

- Qanun 11/2002 stipulating requirements for Islamic dress (*Wajib Tutup Aurat*)
- Qanun 12/2003 prohibiting the consumption and sale of alcohol
- Qanun 13/2003 prohibiting gambling
- Qanun 14/2003 prohibiting close proximity between unmarried or unrelated couples (*khalwat*)
- Qanun 7/2004 setting the guidelines for charitable payments (*zakat*)

In order to oversee the implementation of the Special Autonomy Law, a religious police force was to be established, consisting of 2,500 personnel, recruited from young men studying in Islamic schools and institutions (Galpin 2002). This force was to be financed by the central Indonesian government. Under Qanun 11/2002, it was announced that an Islamic dress code in some areas in Aceh would take effect from March 15, 2002 (McCulloch 2002). All government and private offices would be required to install business signs in the Arabic-based Jawi script, which had been out of common use for over a century (Riddell, P. 2005). The law also widened the authority of the religious courts to cover commercial and criminal cases involving Muslims (McBeth 2002). The initial laws did not include *hudud* provisions for punishment of crime, one of the most controversial areas of Islamic jurisprudence. This was to come later.

This lesser control from the centre did not resolve the difficulties between the Indonesian Government and the GAM. A formal peace agreement was signed between the Acehnese rebels and the Indonesian government on 9 December 2002, recognising partial autonomy and free elections in exchange for rebel disarmament. The agreement broke down in May 2003, with GAM rebels refusing to hand in their weapons, and the Indonesian army not withdrawing to agreed defensive positions. The Indonesian government thereupon declared martial law in the province. GAM launched a third phase of military operations against Jakarta control in a grab for greater freedoms. In response, President Megawati Sukarnoputri (2001-04) increased troop strength in Aceh and launched a military offensive against GAM in 2003 and 2004.

However, the event which precipitated dramatic and rapid change was the December 2004 tsunami, which killed an estimated 175,000 people in Aceh. In the wake of this natural disaster, GAM ceased military operations to focus on recovery (Miller 2006, p. 310), and on 15 August 2005 a formal peace agreement was signed between GAM and the Government of Indonesia, opening the door to greater Acehnese autonomy.

Aceh provides an excellent example of the creeping nature of Shariah legislation; once triggered, it tends to expand in its region of operations and application.

In 2009 a Qanun on Criminal Procedure (*Qanun Hukum Jinayat*) was passed, establishing a new procedural code for enforcement by police, prosecutors, and courts in Aceh. In 2014, a Qanun on Criminal Law (*Qanun Jinayat*) related to newly designated criminal offenses: *ikhtilat* (intimacy or mixing), *zina* (fornication), sexual harassment, rape, and homosexual conduct.

The 2014 *Qanun Jinayat* strengthened penalties for the various crimes, with 60 lashes set for "intimacy", up to one hundred lashes for engaging in homosexual conduct or adultery by unmarried persons, and death by stoning for adultery by a married person.

In the first full-year of implementation of Aceh's Shariah Criminal Code after it went into effect in September 2015, 339 people were lashed in 2016 (Kine 2017). Moreover, the environment of increasing moral strictness translated to specific manifestations, such as a ban on women straddling motorcycles, which was seen as immodest, and a ban on outdoor music concerts in West Aceh regency in April 2016 (Topsfield 2016).

Stage 7: New leadership tries to apply the brakes

The next stage of the Shariah trajectory as seen in our chosen case studies of Egypt and Pakistan is represented by new political leadership which attempts to apply the brakes to the Shariah train.

In Egypt, President Anwar Sadat was assassinated in October 1981 by an Islamist group outraged by his peace treaty with Israel. He was replaced as President by Hosni Mubarak, who was to remain in power for the next thirty years. He set out to reduce the influence of Islamist movements and to attempt to restore national unity, which had been severely damaged by growing Muslim-Christian tensions resulting from the increased influence of Shariah legislation.

Hardline Islamist groups such as al-Gama'a al-Islamiyya (Islamic Group) and al-Gihad (Holy Struggle) were targeted, with many members of both held in administrative detention under emergency legislation; some others such as Ayman al-Zawahiri, who later rose to the position of second in command under Osama Bin Laden in al-Qaeda, fled Egypt to take part in jihad activities abroad. The more mainstream Islamist Muslim Brotherhood was placed under close scrutiny by the Mubarak regime, which set out to thwart its ambitions at every turn. Nevertheless, while the momentum had swung away from those groups who were pushing an overt Shariah-based agenda, their voices in opposition were loud, with the Muslim Brotherhood continuing to undermine interreligious relations with comments such as 'Allah prohibits treating [infidels] in the spirit of Al-Walaa [loyalty] – whether openly or in private – except when one fears them' (Middle East Media Research Institute 2008).

The champion of creeping Shariah in Pakistan, President Zia-ul Haq, also died a violent death in 1988 in a suspicious plane crash. His successor as President, Benazir Bhutto, was head of the Pakistan People's Party, which won a huge victory in the November 1988 elections. She served twice as Head of State (1988-1990, 1993-1996) and struggled to slow down the Shariah train which had been set in motion by her predecessor, Zia-ul Haq, and her own father, Zulfikar Ali Bhutto. Her erstwhile rival, Nawaz Sharif of the Pakistan Muslim League, served as President between her two tenures and subsequent to her second period as President. The Islamisation process increased under his presidency (Lau 2010, p. 402). In October 1990 the Federal Shariah Court ruled that 'the penalty for contempt of the Holy Prophet ... is death and nothing else'. In May 1991 the Enforcement of Shariah Act was passed declaring that 'the injunctions of Islam ... shall be the supreme law of Pakistan'. In 1994 the Lahore High Court extended the application of the blasphemy law to relate to defiling the names of 'all the true prophets of Allah mentioned in the Koran', including Abraham and Jesus. In 1999, a court order instructed the government of Pakistan to change the banking system to an Islamic interest-free system by 30 June 2001.

In 1999, the Pakistani military carried out a coup d'état, installing General Pervez Musharraf as President. Like Mubarak in Egypt (who was also a former military officer) Musharraf was wary of the influence of Islamist forces and sought to slow down the Shariah train and to soften the blasphemy laws to eliminate widespread abuses. But his efforts were thwarted by implacable opposition from Islamist organisations which had been empowered by two decades of creeping Shariah.

However, in the case of Aceh, Shariah laws have not yet been in place long enough in the province to produce a clear backlash and unearth a new leader who tries to apply the brakes, as we have seen in Egypt and Pakistan.

Stage 8: The Blossoming of the Radicals

The purpose of this paper is not to record the recent political history of Egypt, Pakistan, and the Indonesian province of Aceh. It is rather to record a process which all three case studies underwent in the twentieth and early twenty-first centuries, leading them to a place where Shariah law has been significantly empowered in the present day.

In the cases of Egypt and Pakistan, history records that both President Mubarak and President Musharraf lost power in 2011 and 2008 respectively, and both were brought to trial under pressure from their Islamist opponents. In Egypt, the Muslim Brotherhood formed a government following the national elections of 2012 and moved swiftly in the direction of strengthening the role of Shariah law in the structure of state. However, the Muslim Brotherhood led by President Mohamed Morsi only lasted for one year before being overthrown in a military coup d'état.

In Pakistan, frustrated at the level of national politics, an alliance of religious parties (MMA) won power in the parliament of the North West Frontier Province in 2002 and promoted a Shariah-based conservative political program. In June 2003 Islamic Shariah law became the supreme law in NWFP, with the Qur'an deemed to be the source of guidance for all future legislation and reforms in the NWFP (*Institute Condemns Imposition of Sharia Law in North West Frontier Province of Pakistan* 2003). However, the MMA lost control of that province's parliament after a decade in power, being replaced by a Pakistani Movement for Justice (PTI) party advocating an egalitarian modern Islamic welfare state (Rehman 2016).

At the time of writing, the national political stage in both Egypt and Pakistan is a scene of bitter contestation between Islamist and secularist/military interest groups. A key characteristic of this latter stage of the Shariah trajectory is the blossoming of radical Islamist groups, who are willing to use violence to achieve their ends. This is a direct result of the promotion of Islamisation by earlier political leaders, which created a situation where radical groups at the grassroots level could flourish. An essential instrument in this process is the network of madrasas, or Muslim seminaries, a number of which are taken over by radical groups with charismatic leaders who then through their teaching produce the next generation of violent jihadists (Goldberg 2000).

Again Aceh is at an earlier point on the creeping Shariah trajectory, but there are signs of the flourishing of a radical Islamist sentiment, as discussed in the following section.

The Christian experience under creeping Shariah

Our discussion of the Shariah trajectory in eight stages has made passing reference to the experience of religious minorities under creeping Shariah. Our study would benefit from a closer consideration of this issue, with a particular focus on the experience of Christians living under increasingly Islamised societies over the last forty years.

In the case of Egypt, although the Egyptian Constitution guarantees freedom of belief and freedom to practice religious rites, the Government placed clear restrictions on this right, and it is against the law to propagate any religion other than Islam to Muslims. Furthermore, the chaotic Egyptian bureaucracy meant that central authorities in Cairo controlled by President Mubarak often did not have control over the attitudes and actions of local government authorities in far-flung regions.

Authorities from the State and the churches have long been at loggerheads over the question of demographics. Egyptian Christians have frequently claimed their numbers were far greater than the official government figures (Youssef 2002). Churches are not allowed to conduct official censuses so their entreaties to government for a greater say in matters of state have gone unheard.

Christians have suffered discrimination in state employment, being under-represented in senior government positions. Few Christians held senior positions in the military, police or diplomatic services. They suffer from discrimination in the education system. All state school pupils are required to memorise Qur'anic verses as part of their Arabic studies. Christians are barred from teaching Arabic because it is seen as being based on the language of the Qur'an.

In matters of the public media, Egyptian TV broadcasts many Muslim programmes, but none have a specifically Christian content. On the question of churches, any construction or repair of Christian churches required authorisation of high level authorities; bureaucratic impediments mean a low success rate. Furthermore, churches cannot be built near mosques, but this ban is not reciprocal. Islamic activists, when hearing a church was going to be built, have been known to convert a nearby property to a mosque, which then forestalls the church construction (1992 US State Department country report for Egypt cited in Human Rights Watch 1994, p. 12).

Such institutional discrimination can easily lead to active intimidation and persecution. The situation for Christians is particularly difficult in Upper Egypt, where Copts have long been subject to threats by Islamic activist groups which are out of sight from the monitoring of Cairo-based security forces. Human rights agency reports over the last forty years have clearly recorded a worsening situation for Christians and other religious minorities in Egypt (Mohieddin, El Adl & Mohsen 2013), with creeping Shariah legislation privileging Islam as a faith and Muslims as citizens.

The situation in Pakistan is little different from that described for Egypt in the paragraphs above. Creeping Shariah poses challenges to religious minorities, including Christians, wherever it is taking place. For Pakistan, we will limit our comments at this point to the problem of trumped-up blasphemy charges.

The strengthening of the Pakistan Penal Code in 1986 via Section 295C has led to thirty years of increasing charges of blasphemy (Julius 2016). Christians are not alone in falling victim to trumped-up charges of blasphemy; other religious minorities, including minority Muslim groups of Shi'ites and Ahmadis, have also been specific targets. Again, reports detail a typical train of events, where a personal grudge can easily lead to a Muslim citizen charging a non-Muslim with blaspheming the Qur'an or Muhammad. Many people thus charged languish in prison for lengthy periods; some have been murdered in prison, and others have been murdered by vigilante groups, even after such charges were dismissed (Riddell, P. 2009; 2010, p. 7). When religious cases are brought to court, Islamist activists often pack the court room, making public threats against an acquittal. So judges and magistrates often continue trials indefinitely, and the accused is burdened with further legal costs and repeated court appearances.

Where Shariah is being empowered, increasing blasphemy charges are among the most common manifestations of the rising Shariah phenomenon. Of course, not all Muslims wish to empower Shariah; indeed, public opinion surveys suggest at least as many opposed as in favour of strengthened Shariah legislation. In Pakistan, Muslim modernist voices can be clearly heard sounding the alarm bells about creeping Shariah. For example, Abid Hassan Minto, President of the Supreme Court Bar Association, commented: 'The zealots are gaining power, and the judiciary and criminal justice system may not be strong enough to resist them' (Scott-Clark & Levy 1999).

The rise of Shariah legislation in Aceh since the early years of the twenty-first century has shown clear signs of negative impact on Christian residents in Aceh. On the one hand, statements of reassurance are issued, such as the following by Syahrizal Abbas, head of the Shariah legal department in the provincial government: 'Non-Muslims can choose whether to be tried under sharia law or the regular Indonesian criminal code' (Munawir 2015, para. 3). But in a climate of rising Islamic sentiment embedded within an empowered Shariah environment, Christians are feeling the pressure in different ways.

On April 13, 2016, a Christian woman in Aceh was caned for selling alcohol (The Straits Times 2016). The sixty-year-old woman was caned thirty times in the presence of hundreds of onlookers. This case demonstrates the potential for Shariah legislation to overflow beyond Muslim community boundaries.

Furthermore, with Shariah's restrictions on the construction of houses of worship of faiths other than Islam, pressure has been applied on Christian churches. In October 2015, only one month after Aceh's Shariah Criminal Code came into effect, Muslim militants demanded that unlicensed churches in the West Acehnese town of Singkel be demolished, citing a lack of building permits. On 13 October two churches were attacked and burned down by a Muslim mob and at least one person was killed. Police then demolished the remnants of the church with axes and sledgehammers on the morning of 19 October (*Indonesian authorities demolish churches in Aceh* 2015). The Christian community involved then erected tents to use for worship but even these need a permit from the Acehnese authorities and are difficult to obtain.

Conclusion

Our study of what we have termed the Shariah trajectory can be used as both a diagnosis and a prognosis. We have set out to draw on the recent history of Egypt, Pakistan and the Indonesian province of Aceh to identify the process whereby all three communities have moved from predominantly non-Islamist liberal democratic or socialist foundations fifty years ago to a situation today where Shariah law is on the march.

A certain pattern has been identified in our case studies. The Shariah trajectory seems to have followed eight stages, beginning with an awareness of past Islamic glories that were lost and ending in the modern day with bitter contestation within the communities concerned about the place of Islam within the state, especially in the cases of Egypt and Pakistan.[4] In all three cases, a taste of Shariah seems addictive for many; once savoured, more and more is wanted. While some Muslims see Shariah as the antidote to Muslim societies' ills which derive from previous colonial domination, others see Shariah as a kind of Frankenstein that, once let loose, is difficult to control. Such is the diagnostic element to our study.

As for a prognosis, this study calls for further research into the relevance of the eight stages of the Shariah trajectory to other Muslim-majority societies. Do these same principles apply in countries such as Iran, Bangladesh, Turkey and Malaysia? Can lessons be learnt from the Egyptian, Pakistani and Acehnese examples to prevent other Muslim societies experiencing the same kinds of challenges that seem to be the cause of great social disharmony? What does creeping Shariah mean for the future of majority-Muslim societies, as well as for Muslim minorities in the West?

References

Aceh Peace Process Follow-Up Project. 2012. Helsinki: Aceh Peace Process Follow-Up Project.

Al-Attas, S.M.N. 1988. *The Oldest Known Malay Manuscript: A 16th Century Malay Translation of the 'Aqa'id of al-Nasafi*. Kuala Lumpur: University of Malaya.

Berger, M. & Sonneveld, N. 2010. 'Sharia and national law in Egypt', in JM Otto (ed.), *Sharia Incorporated: A Comparative Overview of the Legal Systems of Twelve Muslim Countries in Past and Present*, Leiden: Leiden University Press.

Browne, H.A. 1907. *Bonaparte in Egypt and the Egyptians of To-Day*. London: T. Fisher Unwin.

Carvalho, J-P. 2009. *A theory of the Islamic revival*, Oxford: University of Oxford, Working Paper no.424, https://www.economics.ox.ac.uk/research/WP/pdf/paper424.pdf

The Constitution of the Islamic Republic of Pakistan, National Assembly of Pakistan, http://www.na.gov.pk/uploads/documents/1333523681_951.pdf.

---

[4] The rise of Shariah is more recent in Aceh; we therefore await the emergence of a powerful anti-Shariah movement among the Acehnese, as has been seen in our other case studies.

Effendy, B. 2003. *Islam and the State in Indonesia*, Singapore: ISEAS.

Eighty-Eight Years On, Muslim Brotherhood Stands Steadfast As Ever – for Freedom, Reform, viewed 29 December 2016, http://www.ikhwanweb.com/article.php?id=32483&ref=search.php

Fahmy, K. 1998. 'The Era of Muhammad 'Ali Pasha, 1805-1848', in MW Daly (ed.), *The Cambridge History of Egypt: Vol. 2, Modern Egypt from 1517 to the end of the twentieth century.* Cambridge: Cambridge University Press, pp. 139-79.

Galpin, R. 2002. *Aceh heralds Islamic law*, viewed 29 December 2016, http://news.bbc.co.uk/2/hi/asia-pacific/1874489.stm

Gershoni, I. & Jankowski, J.P. 1987. *Egypt, Islam, and the Arabs: The Search for Egyptian Nationhood, 1900-1930*, Oxford University Press.

Goldberg, J. 2000. 'Inside Jihad U.; The Education of a Holy Warrior', *The New York Times Magazine*, June 25.

Green, A.H. 1980. 'A comparative historical analysis of the Ulama and the state in Egypt and Tunisia', *Revue de l'Occident musulman et de la Méditerranée*, vol. 29, no. 1, pp. 31-54.

Human Rights Watch. 1994. *Egypt: Violations of Freedom of Religious Belief and Expression of the Christian Minority*, Report, Vol 6, no. 2.

Ibrahim, S.E., Tadros, M.R.I, El-Fiki, M.A. & Soliman, S.S. 1996. *The Copts of Egypt*, An MRG International Report 95/6, http://minorityrights.org/wp-content/uploads/old-site-downloads/download-111-The-Copts-of-Egypt.pdf.

Inaugural address by Syed Mawdoodi, viewed 29 December 2016, https://jamaat.org/en/jamaatOrDawat.php?cat_id=11

Indonesian authorities demolish churches in Aceh 2015, viewed 30 June 2017, http://www.bbc.com/news/world-asia-34570570

Institute Condemns Imposition of Sharia Law in North West Frontier Province of Pakistan. 2003. Institute on Religion and Public Policy, March 25, Press Release.

Islam and the State under Nasser, viewed 29 December 2016, http://www.islamopediaonline.org/country-profile/egypt/islam-and-nation-building/islam-and-state-under-nasser

Julius, Q. 2016. 'The Experience of Minorities under Pakistan's Blasphemy Laws', *Islam and Christian–Muslim Relations*, vol. 27, no. 1, pp. 95-115.

Keay, J. 2010. *The Honourable Company: A History of the English East India Company*. London: HarperCollins.

Kine, P. 2017. *Indonesia's Aceh Authorities Lash Hundreds Under Sharia Statutes: Repeal of Discriminatory, Brutal Bylaws Long Overdue*, viewed 30 June 2017, https://www.hrw.org/news/2017/02/08/indonesias-aceh-authorities-lash-hundreds-under-sharia-statutes

Lau, M. 2010. 'Sharia and national law in Pakistan', in JM Otto (ed.), *Sharia Incorporated: A Comparative Overview of the Legal Systems of Twelve Muslim Countries in Past and Present*. Leiden: Leiden University Press.

Liow, J.C. 2015. *The Arab Spring and Islamist activism in Southeast Asia: Much ado about nothing?*, Brookings Institution, Massachusetts, Working Paper, https://www.brookings.edu/wp-content/uploads/2016/07/Southeast-Asia_Liow-FINALE.pdf.

Malik, J. 2008. *Islam in South Asia: A Short History*, Leiden: Brill.

Mansfield, P. 1972. *The British in Egypt*. Holt, Rinehart and Winston.

Maududi, S.A.A.L. *The Islamic Law & Constitution*. Lahore: Islamic Publications.

McBeth, J. 2002. 'The Case for Islamic Law', *Far Eastern Economic Review*, August 22, pp. 12-5.

McCulloch, L. 2002. *Aceh asks: 'Islamic law for whom?'*, viewed 29 December 2016, http://www.atimes.com/se-asia/DC28Ae01.html

Middle East Media Research Institute. 2008. *Muslim Brotherhood Website: Jihad Against Non-Muslims Is Obligatory*, https://www.memri.org/reports/muslim-brotherhood-website-jihad-against-non-muslims-obligatory

Miller, M.A. 2006. 'What's Special about Special Autonomy in Aceh?', in A Reid (ed.), *Verandah of Violence: The Background to the Aceh Problem*. Singapore University Press, pp. 292-314.

Mohieddin, M.M., El Adl, O. & Mohsen, M. 2013. *No change in sight: The situation of religious minorities in post-Mubarak Egypt*, Minority Rights Group International, Report.

Munawir, R. 2015. *Indonesia's Aceh province enacts Islamic criminal code*, viewed 30 June 2017, http://www.reuters.com/article/us-indonesia-aceh-law-idUSKCN0SI02H20151024

The Muslim Family Laws Ordinance. 1961. viewed 29 December 2016, http://bdlaws.minlaw.gov.bd/print_sections_all.php?id=305

Pakistan Penal Code, viewed 29 December 2016, http://www.pakistani.org/pakistan/legislation/1860/actXLVof1860.html

The Preamble of the Constitution of Pakistan, viewed 29 December 2016, http://pakistanspace.tripod.com/archives/56_00.htm

Rehman, D. 2016. *Imran Khan vows to make Pakistan a welfare state*, viewed 29 December 2016, https://en.dailypakistan.com.pk/pakistan/imran-khan-vows-to-make-pakistan-a-welfare-state/

The Republic of Pakistan, viewed 29 December 2016, http://pakistanspace.tripod.com/archives/62_01.htm

Riddell, P. 2005. 'Islamization, Creeping Shari'a and Varied Responses in Indonesia', in P Marshall (ed.), *Radical Islam's Rules: The Worldwide Spread of Extreme Shari'a Law*, New York & Oxford: Rowman & Littlefield, Lanham, pp. 161-84.

—— 2009. 'The reason the Church in Pakistan is so vulnerable', *The Church Times*, no. 7639.

—— 2010. 'Two Murdered in Pakistan', *Touchstone: A Journal of Mere Christianity*, vol. 23, no. 5, p. 7.

Ruthven, M. 2017. 'Islam's Road to the Modern World', *The Australian Financial Review*, 23 June.

Salim, A. 2008. *Challenging the Secular State: The Islamization of Law in Modern Indonesia*, Honolulu: University of Hawaii Press.

Scott-Clark, C. & Levy, A. 1999. 'Beyond Belief', *Sunday Times Magazine*, 24 January.

Shah, N.H. 2000. 'Law and Religion', *Islam and Christian-Muslim Relations*, vol. 11, no. 2, pp. 243-7.

Sjamsuddin, N. 1985. *The Republican Revolt: A Study of the Acehnese Rebellion*, Singapore: Institute of Southeast Asian Studies.

Tadros, S. 2013a. *The Coptic Church in peril: The Islamization of Egypt and the end of Egyptian Christianity*, viewed 15 September 2013, http://www.abc.net.au/religion/articles/2013/09/15/3848945.htm

—— 2013b. *Motherland Lost: The Egyptian and Coptic Quest for Modernity*. Stanford, CA: Hoover Press.

The Straits Times. 2016. *Christian woman caned in Indonesia's Aceh province for selling alcohol*, viewed 30 June 2017, http://www.straitstimes.com/asia/se-asia/christian-woman-caned-in-indonesias-aceh-province-for-selling-alcohol

Topsfield, J. 2016. *Ban on outdoor music concerts in West Aceh due to Sharia law*, viewed 30 June 2017, http://www.smh.com.au/world/ban-on-outdoor-music-concerts-in-west-aceh-due-to-sharia-law-20160406-gnzvna.html

Umm Mutma'inna. 2002. *Sharia implemented in Indonesia's Aceh*, viewed 29 December 2016, http://www.ummahnews.com/viewarticle.php?sid=2422

Wolpert, S.A. 2005. *Jinnah of Pakistan*, Oxford: Oxford University Press.

Youssef, A.R. 2002. *Egyptian Copts: It's All in the Number*, viewed 29 December 2016, http://english.al-akhbar.com/node/12728

The Iranian Church under the Shadow of Shia Shari'ah

Dr Anthony McRoy

Introduction

Iran is unlike some of its neighbours (e.g. Syria, Egypt) because its historic Christian communities are not part of the dominant ethnic group. A further difference is that whereas Christians were the majority in the latter before the Islamic conquests, in Iran they were always a minority. Both factors impact on our study. Iran is the only country directly ruled by Shia Shari'ah. Around ninety per cent of Iranians are Shia (Curtis and Hooglund, 2008: 118).

Another issue to consider is the impact of Iran's relationship with the West. Saudi Arabia arguably has a stricter rule of Shari'ah (albeit from the Sunni perspective) than Iran, but the former is a close ally of the West, whereas Iran is in conscious conflict with America and Britain. This was seen most recently in Syria where the West and Iran backed opposing sides in the civil war. Bad relations with the West have the potential to negatively impact Iranian Christians.

This paper will examine the position of Christians under Shia Shari'ah in Iran by firstly examining the historical status of Christians as a minority there, and demonstrating that effectively, little changed throughout that history in terms of their being a marginalised community, especially when we consider that until recently, Iranian Christians have been largely members of ethnic minorities distinct from the Persian majority.

1. Iran before the Islamic conquest

At one point, the Sasanian Persian Empire stretched from the Caucasus, including Mesopotamia, both sides of the Persian Gulf (an accurate nomenclature then because of Sasanian dominance) and into India. The dominant religion was Zoroastrianism (Donner, 1981: 168). Late Sasanian ideology held that the monarchy had its foundation in the Zoroastrian religion, and in turn was its defender (Pourshariati, 2008: 324). There is some evidence for periodic, severe, but not systematic persecution of Christians (Ibid.: 348-349). Christians in Mesopotamia may have been the largest single group (Gerö, 2008: 125). Most were Nestorian (Donner, 1981: 168). Following the condemnation of Nestorius and harassment of his proponents in the Roman Empire, Byzantine Nestorians increasingly fled to Persia, where Nestorianism received some State encouragement:

> The Persian Government had opposed Christianity partly because it was the religion of their national rivals, the Romans. But now that Nestorianism had been condemned and Nestorians were seeking refuge in Persia, there was no longer any danger that such a form of Christianity would be a link with an alien power; on the contrary, it would be politically wise to encourage Nestorianism among Persian Christians, so as to alienate them from Christians in the Roman Empire. This was accordingly done, and King Peroz (457-484) gave up persecuting the Christians, except for a persecution in 465. (Vine, 1937: 42-43)

Eventually, the Persian Church became principally or even wholly Nestorian.

2. Iran after the Islamic conquest

The general Persian Christian reaction to the Arab conquest was indifference (Gerö, in Donner, 2008: 130). The Christians were a minority before; they remained so afterwards. Persia's Christians eventually experienced the same dhimmi existence as other minorities in the Islamic State, with restrictions on clothing, employment and church building (Baumer, 2006: 151). The millet system, together with the effects of the policies of Timurlane (1336-1405), the ruthless Muslim conqueror of much of the Middle East and Central Asia, and who waged a brutal sectarian war against the 'Church of the East' which decimated it, may have consolidated the process whereby Persia's Christians became associated with the Syriac language – in contrast to Arabic and Persian – and eventually, with Assyrian communal identity, rather than the multi-cultural Nestorian community that existed before Timurlane's massacres and 'encouragements' to conversion to Islam. Perhaps this was accentuated when Catholic missionaries began work in the sixteenth century, seeking to bring 'schismatics' to the Roman obedience (Vine, 1937: 172; Baumer, 2006: 248). This led to secession and the beginning of the Uniate Chaldean Church, which retains aspects of the traditional Nestorian liturgy and some other matters, but recognises the supremacy of the Roman Pope. This caused the existence of two of the recognised Christian communities in Iran, the Assyrian (Nestorian) and Chaldean (Uniate-RC).

The other recognised Christian community was always ethno-linguistically distinct from the Persians – the Armenians. Armenia has a long relationship with Persia: 'Prior to the third century AD, Iran (Persia) had more influence on Armenia's culture than any other neighbor... In the eleventh century, the Seljuk Turks drove thousands of Armenians to Iranian Azerbaijan, where some were sold as slaves, while others worked as artisans and merchants.' (Boumoutian, 2006: 207) Safavid-Ottoman conflict in the sixteenth century also led to Armenians being moved further into Iran (Ibid.: 209). Sometimes royal favour was bestowed on them, as when Abbas I attended the Armenian Christmas in 1619, and the Shah was even present at the baptism of Armenian children in the Zayanda River (Babaie et al, 2004: 69-70). The Armenian Apostolic (Gregorian) Church was traditionally Miaphyiste (like the Copts or Syriac Orthodox Church). Like the Nestorians, from the sixteenth century they faced Catholic missionaries, who won many converts (Kostikyan, in Floor and Herzig, 2012: 371). The Catholics could operate freely (among Christian minorities) because of Iran's commercial links with the West. Nevertheless, neither the Persian Monarchy nor the ulema tolerated such activity among Muslims (Ibid.: 373). However, by the eighteenth century, toleration of Catholics was curtailed, partly through Gregorian pressure, to the point of Armenians being forbidden by Royal decree to embrace Catholicism (Ibid.: 376).

Thus, sometimes Iran was willing to see minorities change religious or at least distinctive sect identity, but never allowed Muslims to forsake their faith or permitted mission among them. Indeed, there were coerced conversions and other negative actions taken against Christians after Shah Abbas: 'Forced conversions to Islam, discriminatory measures, high taxation, and instances of clerical agitation against the Christian population abound in eyewitness accounts.' (Sanasarian, 2004: 38) This shows how the ulema have often engaged in incitement against Christians, and how the state has conspired in one form or another in sectarian intimidation.

The major event in Iranian history after the Muslim conquest was the rise of the Safavid dynasty. Beginning as a Sufi order in the fourteenth century, it became increasingly militarised, engaging in raids against its enemies (Daniel, 2001: 83). The Mongol invasions had decimated Sunni political centres in Western Asia, allowing for a flowering of Shi'ism (Nasr, 1974: 271). The Safavids established their kingdom in Tabriz in 1501 and Shah Esmail 'announced that the official religion of his kingdom would be Shi'ism...' (Daniel, 2001: 87) Prior to this, it is usually held that Iran was a mainly Sunni country (Ibid.; Nasr, 1974: 273). The effect of this change was not only theological, but also political and national, in that the Shia scholars imported into Iran at this time 'were prepared to transform Shi'ism from a religion of the community to that of the state, proposing significant modifications in political theory and becoming highly equipped to circumvent Ottoman and Uzbek propaganda and ideological expansion.' (Abisaab, 2004: 4) Henceforth, Iranian identity was asserted over against Sunni entities outside their borders.

Internally, efforts were made to produce communal cohesion by conversion to Shi'ism: 'Soon after Shah Isma'il I ascended the throne, he mandated that all regions under Safavid control accept Twelver Shi'ism. His immediate successors also persevered in their efforts to convert Persia's numerous tribal groups and social classes to Twelver Shi'ism...' (Ibid.: 8) Under Shah Abbas I, the motivation of forced conversions of Christians was political, rather than theological, 'to instil a greater measure of cohesion and integration among the empire's populations through conversion.' (Ibid.: 63-64) It follows that to be Iranian – and more specifically, ethnic Persian - is to be Muslim, especially Shia, similar to the way that to be Polish is to be Catholic.

Later religious policies in the Gulf aimed at converting Christians had a similar motive – one that still resonates today: 'European expansion overseas rather than direct Ottoman threat became a pressing issue. The Shah's attempt to curtail European supremacy in the Persian Gulf ...kindled an interest in Islamizing Christian groups which could potentially ally themselves with European powers.' (Ibid.: 81) The nineteenth and twentieth centuries saw Iran become the victim of Russian, British, and subsequently American hegemonies. This particularly affects Evangelicals in the twentieth and twenty-first centuries, who are often linked with US politics because of the perceived influence of American Evangelicals therein, and potentially opens Iranian Evangelicals to the charge of being a fifth column, as well as being apostates.

3. Nineteenth and twentieth century mission

The nineteenth century saw a renewal of Catholic mission, and a new phenomenon, Protestant proselytising, mainly British and American (Baumer, 2006: 253ff; Kidd, 2009: 41ff). Initially, the latter centred on reaching the Nestorian and Armenian communities. Small numbers were won for Protestantism, so that there are Assyrian and Armenian Protestants today (Sanasarian, 2004: 40, 41). Nasser al-Din Shah of the Qajar dynasty reigned from 1848, and allowed Christian mission:

> He also tolerated Christian missionaries so long as they limited themselves to medical-educational activities, and proselytized only among the religious minorities. French Catholics began working with Armenians and Assyrians around Lake Urmiah; they then established more than thirty facilities spread throughout the country. American Presbyterians tended to focus on the north; Anglicans on the south... (Abrahamian, 2008: 40)

Note that toleration of mission was permitted within strict confines – i.e. only within the minority sects, not Muslims. The nineteenth century also saw the emergence of the Bahai sect, which grew out of the Babi movement (Daniel, 2001: 107-108). The significance for our consideration is how they were considered by the Shia ulema: 'Bahais, however, were regarded by the Shi'ite establishment as apostates, technically subject to the death penalty, and they have frequently been targets of clerical fury.' (Ibid.: 108-109) This designation of them as 'apostates' and the consequences of this is relevant to our theme.

The 1905-06 Constitutional Revolution held the prospect of some movement toward a British-style constitutional Monarchy and Parliament, but what is significant is its religious aspects:

> The most important concessions, however, went to Islam in general and to Shi'ism in particular. Shi'ism was declared to be Iran's official religion. Only Shi'i Muslims were to hold cabinet positions. The executive could ban "heretical' books, "anti-religious" associations, and "pernicious ideas.' The judiciary was divided into state and religious courts with the clergy retaining the authority to implement the shari'a in the latter. The legislature was not permitted to pass laws that conflicted with the shari'a. To ensure compliance, the National Assembly was to elect senior clerics to a Guardian Council whose sole task would be to vet all legislation. (Abrahamian, 2008: 48)

Note that Cabinet positions were reserved for Shia – thus marginalising everyone else. The Constitution provided for minority representation in the Grand Majles (Parliament): 'five seats for the religious minorities – two for Armenians, one for Assyrians, one for Jews, and one for Zoroastrians.' (Ibid.: 53) However, a senior mojtahed, Sheikh Fazlollah Nuri, opposed the Constitution because 'Babis, Bahais, and Armenians were scheming to destroy Islam with such heretical innovations as elected parliaments, secular laws, and worst of all, religious equality.' (Ibid.: 53) Hence, pluralistic democracy, as practised in the modern West, was seen as heretical.

4. The Pahlavi dynasty

In 1921, Reza Khan, commander of the Cossack Brigade, marched his troops into Tehran, obliging the Qajar Shah to appoint him successively as Commander of the Army, then Minister of War, and finally Prime Minister by 1923 (Axworthy, 2016: 218). Following a short attempt to declare a republic, 1925-26 saw him seize the throne as Reza Shah, naming his dynasty 'Pahlavi' after an ancient Persian language, demonstrating the nationalist, rather than religious character of his ideology. As part of his nationalist agenda, missionary schools were nationalised (Abrahamian, 2008: 84). Reza had already restricted missionary schools from teaching 'Christian values' (Mathee, in Cronin, 2003: 138). Christian minority schools were also closed, and Armenians were 'denied government jobs and employment', whilst villages with Armenian names were Persianised (Sanasarian, 2004: 38). Village evangelism was forbidden in 1931 (Ibid.: 44). Hence, even under a secularist-nationalist agenda, Christianity was viewed as alien.

Reza was dethroned by the British-Soviet invasion of 1941, being succeeded by his son, Mohammed Reza. Iran essentially reverted to being a British client-state. In his book, Mission for My Country, the last Shah expressed pride that the Constitution gave representation to the religious minorities (Shah, 1961: 169). He also spoke quite positively about the beginnings of American missionary work, noting that many Persian leaders were trained at the US missionary school, Alborz College (Ibid.: 134). However, that published sentiment may have reflected his subjection to Washington. This relationship was a result of the 1953 coup, jointly organised by US and UK Intelligence to overthrow the nationalist Prime Minister, Mohammed Mossadeqh, who had attempted to nationalise the holdings of the Anglo-Iranian Oil Company (now

BP), and wanted to reform Iran into a British-style Constitutional Monarchy (Abrahamian, 2008: 117; de Bellaiguee, 2012: 134; Roosevelt, 1979: 2). Mossadeqh's vision of Iranian identity was of civic nationalism, and he rejected clerical demands to impose the veil or ban alcohol (Azmi, 2004: 66).

Under the Shah's regime of Royal dictatorship that followed Mossadeqh's overthrow, Iran became a police state, characterised by rigged elections, torture of dissidents, and shooting of protestors (de Bellaiguee, 2012: 265). Moreover, this was in the context of Iran being an American client-state, which explains the cries of 'Death to America' during the Islamic Revolution. Since then Protestant churches have suffered 'accusations of spying, fueled by contacts with churches outside Iran' (Sanasarian, 2004: 124). This is important to remember, because Mohammad Reza's reign was comparatively peaceful for minorities (Ibid.: 39, 43, 47; 49). This was even true of the Bahais, despite a grass-roots level pogrom on them in 1955 (Ibid.: 52). In theory, the second Pahlavi promoted communal equality: 'Differences were theoretically nonexistent or of minimum importance; everyone was equal before the law; everyone was welcome into any profession. The sameness of all citizens was reiterated, and every ethnic and religious minority was referred to as Irani first and foremost.' (Ibid.: 56)

The 1979 Revolution killed this concept of co-equal civic identity, since it was self-consciously an Islamic event, and after the March 1979 referendum gave its massive support for an Islamic Republic, Khomeini declared 1 April as the 'first day of God's government' (Algar, 1981: 268). It follows that the ethos, constitution and laws of the Islamic Republic must in some sense originate from God – i.e. from the Shia Shari'ah.

5. Shia Shari'ah and its relation to Iranian law and constitution

The primary bases of Shia fiqh are the Qur'an and Sunnah, but Shia adhere to their own hadith collections. Shia jurists hold that the sources of the Shari'ah are four: the Book, the Sunnah, ijma' ('of the 'ulema of the same period as the Prophet or Imams') and 'aql - reason (Mutahhari, 1980: 10). However, they reject qiyas and ra'y (Mutahhari, 1986-87: 8). Iran designates itself as the 'Islamic Republic', thus defining the ideological basis and orientation of the state, as outlined in Article One of the Constitution: 'The form of government of Iran is that of an Islamic Republic, endorsed by the people of Iran on the basis of their longstanding belief in the sovereignty of truth and Qur'anic justice...' (Iran Chamber Society, n. d.) This is further underlined by Article Two, which states:

The Islamic Republic is a system based on belief in:

> 1. the One God (as stated in the phrase "There is no god except Allah"), His exclusive sovereignty and the right to legislate, and the necessity of submission to His commands;
>
> 2. Divine revelation and its fundamental role in setting forth the laws
>
> ...
>
> 6. the exalted dignity and value of man, and his freedom coupled with responsibility before God; in which equity, justice, political, economic, social, and cultural independence, and national solidarity are secured by recourse to:
>
>> 1. continuous ijtihad of the fuqaha' possessing necessary qualifications, exercised on the basis of the Qur'an and the Sunnah ...

Article Twelve reinforces this by stating: 'The official religion of Iran is Islam and the Twelver Ja'fari school [in usul al-Din and fiqh], and this principle will remain eternally immutable.' The references to 'Twelver Ja'fari' establishes that Iran is an ideological Shi'ite state, guided by Shia fiqh. Hence, the basis on which Iranian law is established is Shari'ah, as emphasised in Article Four:

> All civil, penal, financial, economic, administrative, cultural, military, political, and other laws and regulations must be based on Islamic criteria. This principle applies absolutely and generally to all articles of the Constitution as well as to all other laws and regulations, and the fuqaha' of the Guardian Council are judges in this matter.

Article Seventy-two sets the limits of Parliamentary sovereignty:

> The Islamic Consultative Assembly cannot enact laws contrary to the usul and ahkam of the official religion of the country or to the Constitution. It is the duty of the Guardian Council to determine whether a violation has occurred, in accordance with Article 96.

Thus, the Iranian Parliament (Majles As-Shura) is constitutionally restrained from effecting legislation that contradicts Shi'ite fiqh. The 'Guardian Council' is a group of Islamic clerics who effectively operate as Iran's Supreme Court, with the power to over-ride laws issued by the Parliament if they are contrary to Shari'ah, as illustrated by Article Ninety-nine: 'The Guardian Council has the responsibility of supervising the elections of the Assembly of Experts for Leadership, the President of the Republic, the Islamic Consultative Assembly, and the direct recourse to popular opinion and referenda' (Ibid.). Article Sixty-One outlines the purposes of the Judiciary:

> ...the function of the judiciary are to be performed by courts of justice, which are to be formed in accordance with the criteria of Islam, and are vested with the authority to examine and settle lawsuits, protect the rights of the public, dispense and enact justice, and implement the Divine limits [al-hudud al-Ilahiyyah].

The Guardian Council differs from the U.S. Supreme Court in that the latter merely interprets the national constitution in relation to law, whereas the Iranian equivalent interprets Shia fiqh to determine the acceptability of legislation. Essentially Iran has a constitution behind the national constitution - Shia Shari'ah. Of course, only Shia jurists may be appointed to the Guardian Council, thus disqualifying all minorities.

The Iranian Constitution guarantees the rights of the following minorities (Article Thirteen):

> Zoroastrian, Jewish, and Christian Iranians are the only recognized religious minorities, who, within the limits of the law, are free to perform their religious rites and ceremonies, and to act according to their own canon in matters of personal affairs and religious education.

Note that religious liberty in the Islamic Republic is not absolute, in terms of identity and scope. The identity of 'Iranian Christians' is restricted, specifically to the Armenian and Aramaic-speaking minorities (i.e. Assyrians/Chaldeans). This is best illustrated by the references in Article 64 to the specified minority seats in the Majles; they are restricted to 'Assyrian and Chaldean Christians ... and Armenian Christians'. Hence, as far as Iranian law is concerned, to be an 'Iranian Christian' is to be a member of either of these two ethnic groups – Armenians and Assyrians. It follows that an ethnic Persian Christian (effectively, an apostate) is constitutionally impossible and thus unrecognised. That is, he would have no legal protection or rights.

The scope of religious liberty is not limited by incitement to hatred or violence against individuals or communities but rather by

Shari'ah, as enshrined in Article twenty-four, which states: 'Publications and the press have freedom of expression except when it is detrimental to the fundamental principles of Islam...' Hence, it cannot be said that Christians have equal standing with Muslims in Iran; their rights are restricted by Shari'ah. Article Fourteen demonstrates this fact; the government is obliged to treat 'in conformity with ethical norms and the principles of Islamic justice and equity, and to respect the human rights' of those non-Muslims 'who refrain from engaging in conspiracy or activity against Islam...' This concept of good treatment does not apply to those who, even if they desist from terrorism, treason or espionage, engage in acts that contradict Shari'ah, such as proselytising Muslims or converting from Islam. The major Shia hadith collection, Usul al-Kafi, states:

> H 13218, Ch. 46, h 4
>
> Ibn Mahbub has narrated from al-'Ala' ibn Razin from Muhammad ibn Muslim who has narrated the following:
>
> "I once asked abu Ja'far, 'Alayhi al-Salam, about an apostate... He (the Imam) said, 'If one turns away from Islam and rejects what Allah has revealed to Muhammad... after his being a Muslim, his repentance has no effect... executing him is obligatory, his wife becomes stranger to him like an irrevocably divorced woman...'" (al-Kulayni, Vol. 7: 2014: 243)

Rizvi has indicated that apostasy is equivalent to defection or treason, and we must remember that Islam does not separate Religion and State, and that Iran is essentially a theocratic-democracy hybrid:

> In Islam, the concept of treason ...also has a spiritual and cultural dimension to it... open rejection of the fundamental beliefs of Islam by a Muslim is an act of treason... The punishment prescribed by the shari'ah for apostasy is death...
>
> "Murtad" means apostate. Murtad can be of two types: fitri and milli.
>
> (1) "Murtad Fitri" means a person born of a Muslim parent and then he rejects Islam...
>
> (2) "Murtad Milli" means a person who converted to Islam and then later on he rejects Islam...
>
> In the first case, the apostasy is like treason against God; whereas in the second case, the apostasy is like treason against

the Muslim community. Probably, that is why there is also a difference in dealing with these two kinds of murtads:

- A former kāfir who became a Muslim and then apostates (murtad milli) is given a second chance; if he repents, then he is not to be killed.
- But one who is born as a Muslim and then apostates (murtad fitri) he is to be killed even if he repents. His repentance might be accepted by Allāh but he still has to go through the punishment prescribed for his treason in this world.

> This punishment is only applicable in case of apostasy by men; in case of women, the punishment is not death but life imprisonment. And if such a woman repents, then her repentance is accepted and the punishment is suspended. (Rizvi, 1998)

Rizvi quotes a hadith (Furu` al-Kāfi, vol. 7: 257) very relevant to our topic: 'Shaykh al-Kulayni narrates a sahāh hadāth from `Ali ibn Ja`far from his brother (Imam) Abu 'l-Hasan (Musa al-Kāzim) (a.s.). `Ali ibn Ja`far said, "I asked him about a Muslim who became Christian." He answered, "He should be killed and not be asked to seek forgiveness."...' (Ibid.) Rizvi further notes that this is the unanimous view of Shia jurists. Thus, Shia fiqh requires a male apostate to be killed, a female imprisoned, and apostasy occasions automatic divorce. Given that many Iranian Protestants are converts from Islam, their standing in Shari'ah is clear:

> In 1982, for example, Ayatollah Mohammadi Gilani, the judge of the Central Islamic Revolutionary Courts... pointed out that the spilling of the blood of a person who has turned away from Islam "is permissible for anyone who hears of it." In addition to specifying that the criminal should lose his wife and property, Gilani added that in such cases repentance was not acceptable. (Sanasarian, 2004: 130)

Anti-proselytising actions began soon after the Revolution, with missionaries being expelled in 1981, followed by periodic harassment of Protestants: 'The Protestant churches suffered more severe treatment than the Catholic Church partially due to their tendency to proselytize, and also because many of their adherents were Persians.' (Ibid.: 123) A notorious example of this was 'Mehdi Dibaj, arrested in 1983... In 1994 he was brought to trial on charges of apostasy and insulting Islam, and condemned to death.' (Ibid.: 124) Dibaj was both a convert and active proselytiser (Ibid.: 125).

Even apart from apostates, Christians face second-class citizenship in Shia Shari'ah, e.g. in inheritance:

> H 13186, Ch. 37, h 2
>
> Ali ibn Ibrahim has narrated from his father from ibn abu Najran from 'Asem ibn Humayd from Muhammad ibn Qays who has narrated the following:
>
> "I once heard abu Ja'far, 'Alayhi al-Salam, saying, 'Jews and Christians cannot inherit from the Muslims but a Muslim can inherit from Jews and Christians.'" (al-Kulayni, Vol. 7: 2014: 232)

That inheritance and economic factors in Iran are indeed directly affected by Shia Shari'ah is demonstrated by the following case:

> ...two brothers were in conflict over their inheritance from their father. One converted to Islam and married a Muslim woman, thereby winning for himself the entire inheritance. After a long court battle, realizing that the Muslim brother would inherit everything, the other brother also converted, ending up with his half of the inheritance. (Sanasarian, 2004: 131)

A further issue is that the life of a Muslim is not equal to that of a non-Muslim in Shia Shari'ah: '...there is no doubt that there are some differences in shari'a between Muslims and non-Muslims (for example in retribution)...' (Vaezi, 2004: 196) Retribution (qisas) has entered Iranian law as a result of this ruling: 'if a Muslim murders another, he should be killed by the next of kin of the murdered Muslim; if the murdered person is a non-Muslim, then the Muslim cannot be put to death by his kin – punishment through payment of a fine and lashing should suffice...' (Sanasarian, 2004: 25, 132, 133)

Another aspect of Shia fiqh pertinent to our concern is that of Jizyah. According to Muahhari, this tax is considered as tribute – thus indicating a condition of vassalage: 'It is these People of the Book whom we are to fight until they pay the Jezyah (tribute). That is, when they are ready to pay the Jezyah and are humble before us, we are to fight them no more.' (Mutahhari, 1985: 7f) Later, he refers to fighting non-Muslims 'until we subdue them' (Ibid.: 9). Hence, per Shia jurisprudence, non-Muslims are to be subjected to an inferior position in society. However, there is an instance when jizyah is shelved: '...whenever the People of the Book volunteered to come and fight in the ranks of the Muslims in the interests of the Islamic state and the Muslims, the latter didn't collect the jezyah...'

(Ibid.: 65) Since all Iranians perform military service, jizyah has not been imposed in the Islamic Republic. Possibly this reflects the emergency Iran faced when it was invaded by Iraq in 1980, and needed all able-bodied males to act in its defence. However, since the Constitution reflects the Shari'ah, Christians, etc., are considered subjected people, rather than equal citizens.

The Hadith (Al-Kafi) also regards Christians as ritually unclean, such that touching them requires subsequent washing:

> H 3648, CH 11, h 10
>
> Hamid ibn Ziyad has narrated from al-Hassan ibn Muhammad from Wahab ibn Hafs from abu Basir from one of the two Imam, recipient of divine supreme covenant, who has said the following:
>
> "About shaking hands with a Jew or a Christian he had said, 'Shake hands with them from behind clothes and if you shook their hand without clothes then you must wash your hands.'" (al-Kulayni, Vol. 2: 2014: 505-506)

Khomeini's writings demonstrate that he regarded non-Muslims as unclean, along with urine, excrement, dogs and pigs, etc., so we can understand how the theoretical becomes practical in his Islamic Republic (Abrahamian, 1993: 46). For example, 'In one television program, the commentator impudently declared: "A dog, a pig, and a non-Muslim are najess."' (Sanasarian, 2004: 108f) It follows that Christians, etc., are second-class citizens, if they are unclean. This affects non-Muslim places of worship, which are considered unclean. Church buildings are in a precarious position per the Shia hadith:

> H 5280, Ch. 59, h 1
>
> Ali ibn Ibrahim has narrated from his father from Muhammad ibn 'Isa from Yunus from 'Abd Allah ibn Sinan who has said the following:
>
> "I once asked abu 'Abd Allah, 'Alayhi al-Salam, about performing Salat (prayer) in al-Biya' and churches. He (the Imam) said, 'Sprinkle, then perform Salat...' ...'"
>
> H 5199, Ch. 49, h 3
>
> Muhammad ibn 'Isma'il has narrated from al-Fadl ibn Shadhan from Safwan from al-'Is who has said the following:

> "I once asked abu 'Abd Allah, 'Alayhi al-Salam, about al-Biya' and churches if they can be changed into Masjid. He (the Imam) said, 'Yes, it is possible.'"

The famous Shia jurist al-Muhaqqiq al-Hilli (1205 – 1277) demonstrated how the conditions of Jizyah and Dhimmi status affected Christians in terms of church buildings: 'The non-Muslims are not allowed to establish a new church, or ring the naqus (semantron), or to build too high buildings. If they violate this condition, they should be censured (ta'zir). If this condition was stipulated in the covenant, the 'ahd will be considered null and void.' (al-Hilli, 2001: 279) This is reinforced later:

> It is not permissible to embark on rebuilding synagogues and churches in abode of Islam. If they be renewed by someone, they should be obliterated and removed ...
>
> If a church of the latter form, in which they (non-Muslims) are allowed to continue their rituals of worship, is ruined, it is permissible for them to rebuild it (Ibid.: 280).

This ruling also affects endowments for Christian literature: 'If a dhimmi ...wills his money to be spent on inscribing the Torah and Bible... will be invalid since they are both perverted.' (Ibid.: 284) Post-revolutionary Iran banned import of certain religious books that could result in conversion of Muslims (Sanasarian, 2004: 129). This situation continues:

> Iran's non-tolerance of conversion from Islam (apostasy) was articulated publicly in October 2014 by Ali Younesi, Rouhani's senior advisor on Ethnic and Religious Minority Affairs. During an interview with the conservative news agency, Fars, Younesi declared that "Converting to different sects is illegal in our country" and also that evangelism is illegal for minority faith groups. (Christians in Parliament, 2015: 5)

Khomeini, in his treatise Islamic Government written while exiled in Iraq in 1970, expressed intent to destroy buildings of proselytising churches: 'In our own city of Tehran now there are centers of evil propaganda run by the churches... in order to lead our people astray and make them abandon the ordinances and teachings of Islam. Do we not have a duty to destroy these centers that are damaging Islam?' (Khomeini, 2002: 115) Sansarian states: 'At the outset of the Revolution, however, there was no significant destruction or confiscation of churches, temples, or synagogues.' (Sanasarian, 2004: 75) However, no new legal church buildings have been allowed, and churches have faced closures and restrictions, reflecting Shia Shari'ah:

> Since the 1979 Revolution, the government has not granted a licence for the establishment of a new church organisation or allowed the construction of any church building, Orthodox, Protestant, or other. It has required recognised churches to limit attendance to those who are not from a Muslim background, and to conduct services only in the minority languages of Assyrian or Armenian. Churches have also been closed down, and had leaders arrested, if they refused to comply with these restrictions. (Christians in Parliament, 2015: 6)

The humiliating, inferior nature of Christians under Shia Shari'ah is best expressed in this ruling (which does not seem to have been explicitly incorporated in Iranian law, perhaps because of its standing as 'recommended'): 'It is mustahabb for the Muslim to obligate the dhimmi to go along the narrowest routes.' (al-Hilli, 2001: 280)

To apply for the executive and judicial functions within the state, one must be a Shia (Articles 107-109, 113-115): 'Minorities were denied the presidency, the prime ministership, the ambassadorship, ministerial posts, and top-level military positions.' (Iran Chamber Society, n. d; Sanasarian, 2004: 70) In Shia theology, rule is by the Twelve Imams of the House of Ali, and when the Twelfth, last Imam, Abul-Qasim, 'disappeared' around 873 A.D. – the 'Lesser Occultation' - followed by the 'Greater Occultation', when government by his four deputies came to an end in 941, a problem emerged of legitimate government. During the Safavid dynasty in Iran, notably during the weak rule of Shah Sultan Husayn (1694-1722), the power of the ulema grew so great 'that some openly preached the necessity for the ruler to be, not only a Sayyid, but a mujtahid or senior jurisprudent trained in Ja'fari law.' (Cole, 2002: 59) Essentially, Khomeini's theory of the Guardianship of the Jurisconsult (vilayet i-faqih), the ruling ideology of the Islamic republic, is a development of this. Obviously, this excludes non-Muslims from governance.

Conclusion

There has been a remarkable continuity in the condition of Iranian Christians since the Islamic conquest, even under a secularist regime like that of Reza Shah – they are a marginalised minority. Sometimes, this has moved to direct, state persecution. It is true that Iran compares favourably to Saudi Arabia – where non-Muslim religious activity is prohibited (it is not possible to be a Saudi Christian as persecution is relentless) – and to the self-proclaimed 'Islamic State; - where jizyah and enslavement of non-Muslims has been re-introduced. However, it does not equate to western ideas of religious liberty and equality. This is because, as we have seen, behind the state constitution there is another constitution – the Shia Shari'ah. The latter forbids apostasy, and so Christian converts from Islam – who are usually ethnically Persian – have no legal standing, and face at least the prospect of execution.

Evangelicals are often suspect because of their ties to the West, with whom Iran is in conflict. Further, neither the Iranian government nor people are likely to take seriously Western campaigns on religious liberty when the same Western governments are essentially silent about the far worse treatment of Christians – and to a large extent, Shia – by the Saudis. It follows then, that the best hope for an improvement in the condition of Iran's Christians is détente with the West; Western consistency in condemning abuses by Iran's neighbouring foes; and a new ijtihad by Shia fuqaha to bring fiqh into line with modern notions of religious liberty.

References

Abisaab, R.J. 2004. *Converting Persia: Religion and Power in the Safavid Empire.* London & New York: I. B. Tauris.

Abrahamian, E. 2008. *A History of Modern Iran.* Cambridge: Cambridge University Press.

Abrahamian, E. 1993. *Khomeinism: Essays on the Islamic Republic.* Berkeley; Los Angeles; Oxford: University of California Press.

al- Muhaqqiq al- Hilli Abu al- Qasim Najm al- Din Ja'far ibn al- Hasan. 2001. *Shara'I' al- Islam Fi Masa'il al- Halal wal- Haram*, Volume I. Qum: Ansariyan Publications, trans. by Najafi, Hasan M.)

Algar, H. 1981. *Islam and Revolution: Writings and Declarations of Imam Khomeini (1941-1980).* Berkeley: Mizan Press.

al-Kulayni, Abu Ja'far Muhammad ibn Ya'qub. 2014. *Al-Kafi*, Vol. 7. New York: The Islamic Seminary Inc.

Axworthy, M. 2008, 2016. *A History of Iran: Empire of the Mind.* New York: Basic Books.

Azmi, F. 2004. 'Unseating Mossadeq', in Gasiorowski, Mark J., and Malcolm Byrne (eds.) *Mohammed Mossadeq and the 1953 Coup in Iran.* Syracuse: Syracuse University Press.

Babaie, S., Babayan, K., Baghdiantz-McCabe, I., Farhad, M. 2004. *Slaves of the Shah: New Elites of Safavid Iran.* London: I. B. Tauris

Baumer, C. 2006. *The Church of the East: An illustrated History of Assyrian Christianity.* London: I. B. Tauris.

Boumoutian, G.A. 2006. *A Concise History of the Armenian People.* Costa Mesa: Mazda Publishers.

Cole, J. 2002. *Sacred Space and Holy war: The Politics, Culture and History of Shi'ite Islam.* London & New York: I. B. Tauris.

Curtis, G.E. and Hooglund, E. (eds.). 2008. *Iran: a country study.* Washington: Federal Research Division of the Library of Congress, fifth edition.

Daniel, E.L. 2001. *The History of Iran.* Westport and London: Greenwood Press.

de Bellaigue, C. 2012. *Patriot of Persia: Muhammad Mossadegh and a Very British Coup.* London: Random House.

Donner, F.M. 1981. *The Early Islamic Conquests.* Princeton: Princeton University Press.

Gerö, S. 2008. 'Only a Change of Masters? The Christians of Iran and the Muslim Conquest', in Donner, Fred (ed.) *The Expansion of the Early Islamic State.* Aldershot: Ashgate.

Iran Chamber Society, The Constitution of Islamic Republic of Iran, http://www.iranchamber.com/government/laws/constitution_ch01.php; http://www.iranchamber.com/government/laws/constitution_ch09.php accessed January 2017

Khomeini, Imām. 2002. *Islamic Government: Governance of the Jurist.* Tehran: The Institute for Compilation and Publication of Imām Khomeini's Works.

Kidd, T.S. 2009. *American Christians and Islam: Evangelical Culture and Muslims from the Colonial Period to the Age of Terrorism.* Princeton: Princeton University Press.

Kostikyan, K. 2012. 'European Catholic Missionary Propaganda among the Armenian Population of Safavid Iran', in Floor, Willem and Herzig, Edmund, *Iran and the world in the Safavid Age*. London: I. B. Tauris

Mathee, R. 2003. 'Transforming dangerous nomads into useful artisans, technicians, agriculturalists: education in the Reza Shah period', in Cronin, Stephanie (Ed.) *The making of modern Iran: state and society under Riza Shah*. London & New York: RoutledgeCurzon.

Mutahhari, Ayatollah Morteza, Jurisprudence and Its Principles, (New York: Tahrike Tarsile Qur'an 1980)

Mutahhari, Ayatollah Murtadha. 'The Role of Ijtihad in Legislation', (Translated by Mahliqa Qara'i) Ahlul Bayt World Assembly Journal Vol. 4, No. 2

Mutahhari, Ayatullah Morteza. 1985. *Jihad: (The Holy War and its Legitimacy in the Quran)*. Tehran: The Islamic Propagation Organization.

Nasr, H. 1974. 'Religion in Safavid Persia', Iranian Studies, Vol. 7, Nos. 1-2, (Winter-Spring).

Pourshariati, P. 2008. *Decline and Fall of the Sasanian Empire: The Sasanian–Parthian Confederacy and the Arab Conquest of Iran*. London & New York: I. B. Tauris

Rizvi, S.M. 1998. *Apostasy in Islam*, https://www.al-islam.org/articles/apostacy-islam-sayyid-muhammad-rizvi, accessed January 2017

Roosevelt, K. 1979. *Countercoup: The Struggle for the Control of Iran*. New York: McGraw-Hill.

Sanasarian, E. 2004. *Religious Minorities in Iran*. Cambridge: Cambridge University Press.

Shah, M.R. 1961. *Mission for My Country*. London: Hutchinson & Co.

The Christians in Parliament All Party Parliamentary Group and the All Party Parliamentary Group for International Freedom of Religion or Belief. 2015. *The Persecution of Christians in Iran*. London: Christians in Parliament.

Vaezi, A. 2004. *Shia Political Thought*. London: Islamic Centre of England.

Vine, A.R. 1937. *The Nestorian churches: A concise history of Nestorian Christianity in Asia from the Persian schism to the modern Assyrians.* London: Independent Press.

The Application of Shari'a-Law enforced by regional governments in Indonesia
Reviewed from a Christian-Theological Point of View[1]

Dr Olaf Schumann

The topic of this paper invites several challenges. Since the very beginning of Christianity, Christians, their scribes and priests included, developed a very critical attitude toward anything that was presented as "Law". During the time of Jesus and the first Christian generation, what was known as "Law" was the Torah as presented by Moses, which was accepted in two modes: the written Torah as contained in the *Tanakh*, the Hebrew Bible, and the oral Torah which was called *Halakha*. Its origin was also linked to Moses, but it mainly contained the interpretative discussions of the Jewish scribes.

The written Torah consists of the first five books in the Hebrew Bible, called *Tanakh* by the Jews, an abbreviation of *Torah, Nebi'im wa-khetubim*, i.e. the Torah, Prophets and Scriptures. For Christians, it became the Old Testament, or the First Testament. But besides the written Law there existed also in the time of Jesus, as mentioned already, an oral Law or a Law which was practiced and its details discussed by the Jewish scribes. *Halakha* actually means "the way", in Greek *hodos* (ὅδος), and in Arabic *Shari'a* (شريعة). Because the oral Law was also considered to originate from Moses, its authority was quite unchallenged.

But the critique of Jesus was mainly directed against this oral Law and the scribes who determined its contents. He accused them of twisting the original meaning of the written Torah and adjusting it to their own understandings, desires and needs. By using their power and authority, they even sharpened and added more rules to some of its commandments so that obedience then became an increasingly heavy burden to the people. The Torah, if followed according to the precepts of the scribes, was no longer the guidance

---

[1] This article is partly a translation, at some parts a paraphrase with some additions from my article "Penerapan Perda Syariat Islam dikaji dari Sudut Teologi Kristen", as printed in Favor A. Bancin (ed.), *Diskursus Hubungan Agama dan Negara*. Jakarta: BPK dan PGI 2014, pp. 152-165.

and the help (the original meaning of Torah) to facilitate life in this world and make it enjoyable so that God may be praised because of His grace. Instead, the opposite was the case. Jesus' question was whether the Sabbath was established by God and for the sake of humans or whether it was established for the sake of God's majesty. That was the point of his critique. The scribes obviously did not understand the purpose of God's demands and the meaning of the Torah. They made the Torah into their own likeness.

This comprehensive and sharp critique by Jesus was continued and further developed by the apostle Paul. The Torah (or in Paul's Greek term which he adopted from the Septuaginta², *nomos* [νόμος]) which was given by God as a guideline for the way in which to live life together with Him, had been reversed to become a way which in the end led towards death. With the additional obligations of the Law which they forced upon the believers, the scribes made it impossible for a believer to obey and fulfil its demands. On the part of the ordinary Jews, it was believed that whoever did not fulfil the demands of the Torah would have no access to life with God and therefore was prone to punishment or death. That is why Paul said that the Torah, instead of being a means of enjoyment among the believers, became a means of human coercion and suppression.

With this understanding, Paul's teachings in no way attacked the Torah as it was originally intended by God. The goal of his critique was that the Torah was perverted by self-confident scribes who added obligations that were difficult to obey. From this standpoint, Paul developed his theology to counter teachings that stood against the gospel and were in line with this legalistic understanding of the Torah. Thus, Paul's gospel (the εὐαγγέλιον or joyful message) was offered as another way, the new way to life which God had opened and offered by His grace to those who are ready to believe in Him.

From this understanding, any formulation about a "religious law", be it the Torah or the *hodos* or *Shari'a* which establishes rules and laws with the intention to make them into a *lex* (*qānūn*), a legal obligation which has a religious connotation and purpose, e.g. to help obtain salvation, becomes obsolete in the understanding of Christians. In other words: there is no place in Christian understanding for a religious law which would imply that it is relevant for salvation.

---

² This is mainly a Greek translation of the Hebrew Bible accomplished by Jews living in Alexandria during the 2nd century before Christ.

It should be added that in the history of Christianity, the church often trespassed this belief. Therefore, when I critique any understanding of "religious law" as being tantamount to faith, I refer not only to religions beside my own, but include it as well. In Christianity (in mainly the Catholic tradition), there has always been a strict terminological distinction between legal matters concerning the church as *sacerdotium*, and those concerning the state as *regnum*. For example, the church had no direct access to enforce capital punishment. Whenever she felt that that punishment was necessary she had to transfer such a case to the *regnum*. On the other hand, the *regnum* had no right to interfere into matters under the rule and authority of the *sacerdotium*.

The Law that was originally given by God as the Torah had already lost its original purpose as guidance which should lead to salvation. This was also caused by the scribes and their perversion of the original Torah with their additions and changes which prevented the believers from following the Torah of God with joy and dedication. According to the impression of many observers, the Islamic *Shari'a* suffers under the same or similar symptoms. Of course, there is a basic difference between the written Torah which is considered as a direct revelation of God, and the Islamic *Shari'a*. *Shari'a* was never considered to be a written text revealed by God. It usually was considered to be a compilation worked on by the scribes through their studies of the Qur'an, which is the only direct revelation, and achieved by their deliberations resulting in a consensus (*ijma'*).[3] These deliberations continued through different times and at different places, and therefore "the" *Shari'a* as a single obligatory text binding on everyone never was, and could never have been achieved. Of course, these deliberations refer to revelation, under its aspect of *shar'* (شرع) which in this context may also mean "revealed directives". But the *Shari'a* itself resulted from the deliberations of the *ulama* (Islamic scholars), and in this respect it resembles the Jewish *Halakha*. It is not only by chance that the basic meaning of both terms is "to walk", to practice life, and in the religious context – it is to lead a life blessed by God.

Again, the *Shari'a* in the beginning was also considered to give guidance, orientation, and wisdom.[4] However, it was corrupted to

---

[3] See my other essay in this volume.

[4] Wisdom originates in both Arabic and Hebrew in the same verbal root, *hikma* or *hokhma*, and the term *hukm*, often referred to as law, has the same origin.

become something like a carriage leading to salvation, and only those may enter it who obtain the permission of the *ulama*, or that of the scribes in Judaism, as if they had the right to determine who may gain salvation and who may not.

Returning to Jesus, it was this understanding of the carriage which excluded all "unbelievers" which he rejected. So the way appointed by God still exists and is available by the presence of Jesus Christ[5]; it was not without purpose that the first Christians were considered those who follow the *hodos* of the Christ[6], instead of the *hodos* of the other teachers. They follow the Christ by using their own feet, not by the means of another carriage. He is the way and guide to the right direction. Those who want to follow him are free to do so, needing no ticket to enter a carriage.

But again, we have to acknowledge that this freedom to become his follower was not always offered by his church. Time and again it was restricted to those who were judged to be appropriate for their journey to salvation; obedience to human dogmas and prescriptions were the criteria for that judgment. We can only hope that such legalism belongs to the past in the life of Christ's community.

Here we face a problem which always reappears whenever a system of religious law is discussed. In our time, some people desire to render such a law as "Divine Law", or "Sacred Law" and the like, in order to underline its sacred character. The authority of the *Halakha* in Jewish tradition was also stressed by aligning it with the highest authority in Judaism, namely, the authority of Moses as its originator. But in Jewish tradition, the *Halakha* was never called the "Divine Law" because it was not revealed; Moses was considered to be its originator. Only something which is directly revealed by God may be called "divine" or "sacred" because only God is sacred, and only God is divine. This is actually also the conviction of the Jews in general, the Christians and also the Muslims.

But in the present day there seems to be a degree of inflation regarding terms like "sacred", "holy" and "divine". Many people claim that the beliefs and practices which they favour are also sacred; religious scholars in particular tend to consider the products of their minds as having at least a sacred touch. However, logically, everything which is composed by humans, even when it is mixed

---

[5] John 14:6.

[6] Acts 14:26.

with divine insights (like the *Halakha* or *Shari'a* being a mixture of statements originating in the divine revelation) are formulated by human beings and mixed with their understandings. To call such mixtures "sacred" is fundamentally a heresy in all three religions.

During my studies of Islam, I have never encountered formulations like "*Shari'a muqaddasa*", or "*Shari'a ilahiyya*" (divine law). Perhaps there exist recent Indonesian or Malaysian *madhabs* (legal schools) that teach such things, but if they are really recent or "new" then they may be also regarded as *bid'at* (heresy) by other groups because they have no legitimation in the traditional corpus of Islamic teaching and in the only text which is acknowledged as revelation (*wahy*): the Qur'an. Regrettably, there are many obvious contradictions between this new *Shari'a* and the traditional understanding (such as Qur'anic verses which concern non-Muslims, or the enforced fasting of pregnant women, sick and old people, travellers etc.).

What are the inherent problems? Firstly, there are several verses in the Qur'an which underline that God never burdens his creatures with something they are unable to bear as God is not a tyrant (Sura 8:51). Secondly, the Qur'an on several occasions, and also the "Treaty of Madina" (which some Muslims consider to be something like a blue-print for any Islamic constitution), explicitly affirm that every religious community which venerates God follows its own religion, *din*, which includes the rules and regulations based on religious teaching.[7]

The Islamic tradition confirms that the *Shari'a* is formulated and compiled by the *ulama*, not even by the prophet. The *ulama* are scholarly human beings devoid of any divine attributes like infallibility. Their source may be, as usually is claimed, the revelation (the Qur'an). Other sources may be the *ijtihad*, i.e. the personal reasoning of a scholar, or the *ijma'* which is the consensus of a number of *ulama*. But these sources, although acknowledged by the Islamic tradition as trustworthy, are based on humans. Therefore, whatever the outcome of their deliberations may be, they are not devoid of the possibility of errors, and, as shown above, even open contradictions with the Qur'an or the generally accepted tradition, the *sunna*, may be agreed upon by certain groups of *ulama*.

---

[7] *Lakum dînukum wa-liya dînî* (QS 109:6, for you your religion and for me mine), where it is even applied to the infidels; see also the "Treaty of Madina", par. 25.

To say that it represents the eternal Will of God is unacceptable, if not a blasphemy.

The weakness of religious scholars based in their character, the often limited scope of their knowledge and wisdom, and their doubtful behaviour in public, was already critically examined by Jesus in the Gospels and in other Christian and non-Christian books of religious authority. Consider an example: when the scribes and others brought a woman to Jesus and asked him to confirm their decision to stone her because she was caught *in flagranti* by committing adultery, and according to their law, she deserved that sentence, Jesus replied: "Whoever of you is without sin may throw the first stone." No-one did, and one by one they disappeared[8]. They were at least honest with themselves.

It may be of interest to point to a similar story narrated in the Hadith and related to Muhammad: "Narrated by ''Aisha: The Quraish people became very worried about the Makhzumiya lady who had committed theft. They said 'Nobody can speak (in favour of the lady) to Allah's Apostle and nobody dares do that except Usama who is the favourite of Allah's Apostle. When Usama spoke to Allah's Apostle about that matter, Allah's Apostle said, 'Do you intercept (with me) to violate one of the legal punishments of Allah?' Then he got up and addressed the people, saying "O people! The nations before you went astray because if a noble person committed theft, they used to leave him, but if a weak person among them committed theft they used to inflict the legal punishment on him. By Allah, if Fatima, the daughter of Muhammad, committed theft, Muhammad will cut off her hand!".[9] Muhammad urged the people to reconsider their decision by using a legal argument (*ijtihad*), thus avoiding a possible accusation that he himself would not be consistent in applying "God's Law".

There are many reports in the Hadith that confirm that Muhammad was quite strict in applying severe punishments, including in cases of adultery. But there are also narratives in which he appears as someone who also recognises the humanity of the culprits. As is reported in one Hadith transmitted by 'Aisha: "Avoid legal punishments from Muslims as far as possible. Whenever there is a

---

[8] John 8:1-8.

[9] *Sahih al-Bukhari* book 81, No. 779. See also Adel Theodore Khoury, *So sprach der Prophet. Worte aus der islamischen Überlieferung.* Gütersloh: G. Mohn 1988, p. 314. (= GTB Siebenstern 385). I am thankful to Prof. Peter Riddell for drawing my attention to this Hadith.

chance then let him escape. It is better for an imam to make a mistake when forgiving then than to make a mistake when punishing".[10] And an illustration to this advice: By Abu Huraira: "A man called Ma'iz al-Aslami came to the Prophet and acknowledged that he had committed adultery. But the prophet turned himself away. That happened three times. After the fourth time the prophet ordered to let him be stoned. But he managed to run away. But then he met a man who carried a bone of a camel. He hit him until he died. This was reported to the Prophet. He said: 'It would have been better if they had let him escape'".[11] "Whenever possible, the Prophet urged for forgiveness and reconciliation" (by Anas).[12]

Medieval and present day judges often seem to have no idea of this religious fundamental. Let us consider our present time: Not long ago the news media reported from Saudi Arabia that a judge had sentenced a young convict to one thousand (!) strokes of the cane because of blasphemy. Would God be happy about that? Elsewhere recently, a female member of the "*Shari'a* police" in Aceh, Indonesia, was reported to have said (after the flogging of a girl accused of having committed *khalwa* or illegal sex), "We started (the introduction of *Shari'a* law) by accustoming the people to it, then in a second phase we emphasized education, and now the time of punishing has come". This statement needs no comment.

The *Shari'a*, like other "religious laws", are human-made and should be acknowledged as such. This is a matter of honesty, in front of God and in front of other human beings. Let us consider another example of how truly religious people deal with "religious law" and the way that religious experts deal with it. When Jesus was asked by a scribe: "Who is closest to me (usually translated as 'who is my neighbour')? who is worthy to be loved according to God's will?", Jesus answered with the parable of the "good Samaritan".[13] A man was robbed and nearly killed and lay beside a public road. A priest and a Levite passed by him avoiding any contact because, according to their religious law, someone who suffered such a fate must be "unclean" and cursed by God. By their definition, this person was a sinner and when dealing with him, his

---

[10] *Ibid.*, p. 315 (Tirmidhi).

[11] *Ibid.*, p. 305 f. (Tirmidhi, Bukhari and others).

[12] *Ibid.*, p. 315 (Abu Da'ud, Nasa'i).

[13] Luke 10:25-37.

"dirt" might pollute them and even transfer the curse. Therefore they had to ignore and abandon that man. Then a Samaritan came and helped him. The Samaritans, in the eyes of the Jews at that time, were, religiously speaking, worse than the heathens, because they as descendants of Israel, had mixed with the "unclean" Assyrians. This "unclean" person helped the nearly dead victim, whom the priest and Levite considered cursed by God. Then Jesus turned the question of the scribe around. He did not answer it but put forward his own question: "So which of these three do you think was neighbour to him who fell among the thieves and was in need?" The scribe had to admit: the Samaritan fulfilled God's demand. For God, human beings and their welfare are utterly important, not a "religious prescription" or "law".

The last example considers God's dealing with Cain who had murdered his brother Abel. God punished him severely because he had brought death into God's creation which God had created for life. But when "mother earth" (in Hebrew *adamah*) had swallowed Abel's blood which demanded blood revenge, God rejected it[14]: He rejects any destruction or mutilation of life He has created to live, and this is His order and law since the beginning of His creation; it is not by chance that this story is mentioned in the first pages of the Bible. Anything which counteracts this fundamental "life order" of God is against Him and His will, including human made stories of wars and other human atrocities where God is said to be involved or even supports and legitimizes them.

What is offered to be the "Law of God" is all too often human made, using quotations from God's revelation and inspiration, but compiled and adjusted by human beings according to their liking. And there is no human being void of sin, although not many dare to acknowledge that, like the guardians of the law who brought that girl to Jesus to condemn her. They are real exceptions. The climax of God's intention with creation is to safeguard life. The anti-climax of the human behaviour is the disrespect for the dignity and integrity of His creatures as expressed in the "Chant of Lamekh" quoted in the same chapter after the story of Cain and pointing to the deterioration of human morals and his character:

---

[14] Gen. 4:10,11,15.

Cain shall be revenged seven times;

But Lamekh seventy seven times! [15]

To claim that God legitimizes the mutilation of any of His creatures which He created, or even causes its destruction or annihilation is a direct assault on the Creator and His Wisdom.[16] God is here described as having the mentality of a human, He is described according to the image of the human, and this is an attack on the Second Commandment.

Neither the Bible nor the Qur'an are books of dogmatic teachings, even when the Qur'an is believed by Muslims to be a direct revelation by God. It is a book that teaches faith, a *hidaya* (guidance) to faith, a *furqan* or discerning between truth and falsehood. Dogmatics, and likewise written law, are products of human consideration and deliberation. The early church, and also the first generation of the followers of Muhammad, knew that the text of Holy Scripture has to be explained or interpreted. In Islam, the first one to do so was the prophet himself. If the written revelation could answer every question, then the explanations which were later collected in the Hadith would not have been necessary.

The traditional *ulama* of the Islamic *umma* (community) were actually quite aware that the only thing which could claim to be of universal and perennial value was the revelation itself. Even the acceptance of an *ijma'*, the consensus of the scholars, one of the acknowledged sources of Islamic Law, was regionally and temporarily limited. That could not be different, because any law if it is claimed to be relevant must be contextual. Therefore, in Sunni Islam, not only one but four different schools of law (*madhab*) are accepted as being "orthodox", and *madhab* again means "a way". Especially in their details (*furu'*, branches), they may differ quite basically.

But the problem of *Shari'a* is not only linked to the scholars, be it their standard of knowledge, their wisdom, and their personal integrity. More problematic is its use, or misuse, by rulers and political leaders who have tended to use it for their personal prestige or benefit. Recognizing this danger for the integrity of any religious

---

[15] Gen. 4:24.

[16] Another story which emphasizes the human will to destroy against God's will to save is the story of Jonah, see Jonah 4:1 ff.

exposure for the welfare and stability of any community, the eminent Islamic philosophers (beginning with al-Farabi and his book the "Favourable Society", *al-madina al-fadila*)[17] demanded that the caliph be considered the highest authority in the Islamic *umma* as long as they were elected by the *umma*; this followed the example of the first four "rightly guided caliphs" after the death of the prophet. The criteria would be the caliph's ability as a political and religious leader in the area of *siyasa* (politics), and his character as an example for ethical and devotional conduct. Matters of religious impact should be handled by the *ulama* as the experts in this field.

But these concepts found little response in the Muslim world, especially among the rulers who were opposed to them. Only a few of them were in favour, including Nizam al-Mulk, a ruler in the Persian East who was on good terms with al-Ghazzali, the eminent scholar of the 11th century. But when he was murdered, Ghazzali went into exile to Syria. The court scholars accepted the claims of the rulers that their power was given by God to them, that they had to be respected as the "*khalifat Allah*" (vicegerent of God, instead of the original understanding of "*khalifat an-nabi*", successor of the prophet), and thus Islam became "*din wa-daula*", the unity of religion and dynasty.

The rendering of *daula* as "state" rather than as dynasty is common among recent translators of Arabic texts into European languages who intended to give this term a modern image. *Daula* originally means a change, particularly a change from one rule to another one. The first writer who used this term in a broader sense was a Christian convert to Islam, Ali at-Tabari (9th century), who described the "change of rule" (*daula*), or the transfer of rule by God from Christianity to Islam, thus at the same time justifying his conversion.[18] To translate *daula* as "state" is misleading, and to unify religion and politics under the banner of Islam has no basis either in the Qur'an or in the early history of Islam. This statement does not deny that Islam (like Christianity) has a paramount interest in social welfare, social justice, respect of human dignity and clean

---

[17] In this book, al-Farabi further developed ideas forwarded already by Plato and Aristotle by linking it to an Islamic environment starting from the "Society of the Prophet" (*madinat an-nabi*), Further included in this line of philosophers were al-Marwardi and al-Juwaini who were given the title of honour "*Imam al-Haramain*", the proponent of the two sacred places (i.e. Mecca and Madina).

[18] Cf. Olaf Schumann, *Jesus the Messiah in Muslim Thought*. Delhi: ISCPK and Hyderabad: HMI 2002, p. 35 f.

governance; the call to justice cannot be separated from the other aspect of Muhammad's early message: to worship only the One God. To worship God includes all aspects of life. Worshipping Him and at the same time committing injustice is a contradiction in itself. This was actually the starting point of Muhammad's prophetic message which repeatedly stressed that the God-fearing people – in difference to the unbelievers – practise the *"amr bi-l-ma'ruf wa-n-nahy 'an al-munkar"*, obey the order to do what is good and follow the rejection of evil-doing.[19] But this is something different from a direct and active involvement in political affairs with all their iniquities, intrigues and foul play. The prophetic role of religion in the civil society would thus become ossified. This does not mean that a religious person as a citizen may not become a politician. But he should safeguard his personal and religious identity and integrity.

Although the call of the Islamic philosophers did not find much response in their own societies, it was later picked up by European philosophers and thinkers such as Jean Jacques Rousseau and Ernest Renan. Their deliberations about a civil society (remember *madina fadila!*) clearly show, whether they realised it or not, the impact of the Islamic philosophers and their efforts to develop further their philosophical inheritance from the ancient Greeks (mainly Plato and Aristotle). Possibly with more emphasis than the Islamic philosophers, the European thinkers were more eager to stress the distinction and even separation of the realm of the religious and the political spheres, or of *sacerdotium* and *regnum*, with respect to the rulers and their relations to the pope and bishops.

These institutions were not known in the Islamic tradition, although the *Shaikh al-Islam* in the Ottoman Sultanate, and not the Sultan and Caliph, was, constitutionally speaking, the religious leader, and the Sultan and Caliph had no formal power to decide about the person who obtains this office.[20] Usually, the *Shaikh al-Islam* was, before taking over this office, the Grand Mufti of Constantinople (Qustantiniyya), the capital city of the empire, and his position in

---

[19] QS 3: 104, 110; 7:157; 22: 41 and many other verses.

[20] When, as an example, the Ottoman Sultan Abdulhamid II tried to extend his authority into the field of religious administration he was rebutted; see below. Religious matters were supervised by the *Shaikh al-Islam*, and he was the representative of the religious scholars (*'ulama*).

the hierarchy of power was equal to that of the Grand Wezir.[21] Since the Ottoman Empire was understood as implementing the principle of "Islam is *din u devlet"*[22], the administrative body dealing with religious affairs, mainly those of legal impact, was quite voluminous in the sultanate, which strengthened the power of the *Shaikh al-Islam* and the *ulama* under his supervision. However, they did not much interfere into the legal products of the "secular" lawmaking authority of the Sultan and his political aids whenever they enacted necessary *kanuns*. Further, the Sultan had also no power to decide on religious matters, like issuing a *fatwa* even when it had a political impact, like a *fatwa* on *jihād* during World War I.[23] The Sultan and Caliph was the political leaders. Even Sultan Abdulhamid II during the last decades of the 19th century could not dismantle the religious authority of the *Shaikh al-Islam*. The Young Turks tried to endow the Caliph with religious authority, but after the abolition of the Ottoman Sultanate in 1922, this was a complete failure. After two years the "religious Caliph" they had installed was also dethroned.

This is quite different compared to the situation in Indonesia where the members of the *Majelis Ulama Indonesia* (MUI) are considered to be the highest authority of the Islamic community and a "partner" of the government. But they are appointed by the government, and not by representatives of the *'ulama* or even the *umma* as is the case with the other religious communities (i.e., Buddhists, Christians) and their highest representatives in Indonesia.[24] It is not our task to evaluate the position and authority of the *Majelis Ulama Indonesia* among their *umma*. Here, we should note that in Islam, the distinction between political and religious affairs is not something

---

[21] Josef Matuz, *Das Osmanische Reich. Grundlinien seiner Geschichte*. Darmstadt: DGW , 2nd ed. 1990, pp. 89, 92 ff.

[22] This is the Tukish version of the Arabic *"din wa-daula"*, Religion and Dynasty. See Binnaz Torprak, *Islam and Political Development in Turkey*. Leiden: E.J. Brill 1981, p. 30.

[23] See my article on "Jihad for whom? The Radicalization of Religion as a Response to Political Oppression. From Turkish to Indonesian Islam", in: *Journal of Indonesian Islam*, vol. 2, 2008, 240-266; an enlarged Indonesian version in Olaf Schumann, *Agama-agama, Kekerasan dan Perdamaian*. Jakarta: BPK 2011, 2nd print 2015, pp. 189-232.

[24] It is worth noting that the "Persekutuan Gereja-gereja di Indonesia" (PGI, Community of [Protestant] Churches in Indonesia) was established by its member churches while the "Konperensi Waligereja Indonesia" (KWI, [Catholic] Conference of Bishops in Indonesia), and similarly the representative bodies of the Hindu, Buddhist and Confucian communities are established by their respective members; all of them are rooted in their respective communities. They are acknowledged by the Government as to be the representative bodies for their own religious communities and are furnished with their respective departments in the Ministry for Religious Affairs.

unknown, although the dependence on the political authority is sometimes quite strong. There exists, however, a particularity in Islam. "Theology" (*'Ilm al-Kalam*) as a branch of the sciences stands beside Jurisprudence (*'Ilm al-Fiqh*), but matters of religious order like liturgy, fasting, prayer, pilgrimage etc. are, as *'Ibadat*, a branch of Jurisprudence.

The Bible and the Qur'an do not offer any blueprint for any kind of government, constitution or composition of a society. What they offer and underline are guidelines for values, principles for ethics, social solidarity, and justice, for responsibility and truthfulness among each other. The ideal is a prosperous, well-balanced and harmonious society without discrimination, marginalisation, and suppression of either groups or individuals, void of any acts which attack the dignity and status of anyone, which stigmatise those "different" from what is considered to be "common". Rules and laws are judged according to their truthfulness and honesty, that is, according to the spirit in which they are created and executed and not according to their religious or ideological background.

History has more than sufficiently proven that laws and prescriptions which are said to be rooted in a revelation or other religious authority that are in accordance with the will of God, are susceptible to error and human manipulation. Even the Holy Scriptures and their verses are used by Satan for his purposes.[25] Therefore the origin of these verses is not a guarantee for its correct use. The measure as to whether something is in accordance with God's will or not is, as has been previously mentioned, whether it is in line with His intention to make His creation a place to be enjoyed and loved *by all of its inhabitants.* Any kind of destruction and death-causing, torture, mutilation, egoistic exploitation and other kinds of disruption opposes His will. He created His world that it may live and not to be corrupted by some of His creatures. The religious communities may judge themselves as to how far they are taking these principles seriously, or as to how far they are neglecting them.

There seems to be much idealism behind these statements. Nevertheless, one of the greatest dangers for a decent religious life comes from politicising religion. It is no secret that in such cases, religion can serve as a justification for any kind of atrocities and iniquities which may issue from the human mind. And this mind is mainly concerned with its own well-being, benefit and prosperity. If

---

[25] Luke 4:1-13.

religion becomes a part of this play then it loses any credibility. Therefore, those who take their religion seriously have to be cautious that it may not be mixed up with politics and its methods.

There are some groups in Indonesia and in Malaysia (among the Malays) who continuously complain that Islam has not been given the proper place it deserves in society after political independence was achieved. What they mean is that the Islamic *Shari'a* was not accepted as the basis of the national legislation. In a democratic country – and both countries claim to be democracies – a simple question may be raised: from where do these religious politicians obtain the legitimation to make such a statement? In both countries frequent elections have taken place in which all citizens where invited to vote. One may say, of course, that in Indonesia particularly in the time of Suharto's regime, most elections were manipulated. But in 1955 when the first (and for some time the last) free elections took place both for the *Konstituante* (elected to produce the definite Constitution) and for the Parliament, the "Islamic" parties which called for the replacement of the Pancasila by the *Shari'a* (without explaining how they understood *Shari'a*) altogether obtained about 43.5 percent of the votes. If it were true that the Islamic *umma* makes about 90 percent of the Indonesian nation, then not even half of the *umma* had voted for the *Shari'a*.

In 1999 and 2004, the first elections after the fall of Suharto, only about 16 percent of the voters supported the Islamic parties. This number may be increased by a number of members of other "non-Islamic" parties who are also thought to opt for the *Shari'a* although officially their parties maintain a neutral position. If we add these individuals altogether to those who elect Islamic parties, they total around 37 percent according to several estimations. Looking at these numbers one may ask: on which basis, or with what kind of legitimation do the Islamic politicians claim to speak in the name of the whole *umma*? In a democracy the majority decides, and it is obvious that the majority of the Muslims is not in favour of an Islamic State based on the *Shari'a*. The majority in politics results from the votes cast in an election – it is not a majority based on a poll or census. The majority in politics is the political majority, and not the ethnic or religious one. This was also the understanding of the National Movement in Indonesia in which all groups participated, regardless of their ethnic, religious or social backgrounds. In Malaysia, a strong national movement never existed. Ethnic differences and conflicting interests dominate the political life in that country, and the role of Islam is defined by the Malays and the powerful role of the sultans.

In a poll conducted a few years ago in Indonesia as was reported in the news media, about 77 percent of those questioned definitely resented the application of the *Shari'a* as the basis of any law, including the *"Peraturan Daerah"* (abbreviated as *"perda"*, regional prescriptions). This polling was conducted several months after the *Shari'a* was enforced by the regional government of Aceh. After a series of floggings in 2016 and other unqualified acts against the human dignity of Muslims and non-Muslims alike which continue until the present (July 2017) and which are frequently reported by human rights agencies, the resistance against this politically inspired *Shari'a* is increasing. Many people have started asking: "Who are those people in power to enact such rules which contradict basic religious values, teachings and convictions? Who are they who disregard basic rules of a civilised and civil society and at the same time conflict with the State Constitution and ignore the will of the people?"

Another point is a non-theological one. The sovereignty of a state is based on its sovereignty over the law which is promulgated and practiced in its territory. If it cedes part of its sovereignty to other authorities it becomes a weak state, and consequently a puppet state. That is what frequently happened in the past, not only in Islamic but also in Christian history. Modern states, especially those with a colonial past, usually are eager to maintain their unchallenged sovereignty. That is a matter of self-respect and an obligation towards the people who established it and suffered for its realization. It is highly questionable whether those indigenous rulers now using their unchecked power are entitled to punish their people with laws which are more rigid than those applied during the colonial era.

Nobody would object to Muslims who implement the demands of a *Shari'a* which is based on the genuine values and ordinances of their religion in their daily life. This is because the Constitution also protects the free exercise of religious duties (although it often proves unable to do so because of its manipulations by those in power). The guidelines for social behaviour during the life-time of the prophet were based on principles like "there is no compulsion in religion"[26], "you follow your religion and I follow mine",

---

[26] QS 2:256.

"practicing the good and rejecting the wrong" (*al-amr bi-l-ma'rûf wa-n-nahy 'an al-munkar*).[27] In Madina, however, the situation changed. Economic and political considerations demanded attention. But it was maintained, and later on became a principle for Islamic jurists, that God never burdened the human being with something which he/she is unable to bear (Sura 2:286). The disregard for this basic religious principle is apparent in many of these "regional prescriptions" said to be based on a *Shari'a*. It not only shows a disrespect or ignorance of the basic principles of religion but also points to a basic lack of sensitivity for whatever religion means. Lastly, it reveals a deep contempt for the dignity of human beings.

There are many examples which underline this conclusion. Instead of making religion enjoyable as a source of joy and welfare, of honesty and justice, loving God and the neighbour, it was made into a source of pain, suffering and enmity between different groups, thus inviting hypocrisy and corruption. This is intolerable in a civil society and dishonours the role of religion in it. And it is against any genuine and noble religious message.

---

[27] QS 3: 104, 110; 7:157; 22: 41. But also this guideline may be distorted by the hypocrites, see SQ 9:67.

The Church under the lengthening shadow of syariah in Brunei Darussalam

C.T. and Dr John Cheong

Introduction

In 2014, the tiny country of Brunei Darussalam (henceforth Brunei) made international headlines when it announced that it would introduce syariah law as the supreme law of the land. An international outcry led to governments around the world as well as Western news outlets, rich business people, and movie celebrities announcing their boycott or sale of any property, product or business managed by the Sultan of Brunei or the government (Morris 2014).

While such change is undermining one of Brunei's big draws for investors (a stable legal system based on English law), its impact on its residents on the ground-level, and on its non-Muslim minorities is more palpable, if not threatening in some instances.

This paper will trace the unfolding progress of Brunei's attempts to enact syariah law. It will discuss some key developments in Brunei's history of its Malay and Muslim identity to give a context for how Islam shapes but is also shaped by this dynamic. Thereafter, we will outline areas of concern that relate to Brunei's civil and religious freedom today. This paper will conclude with some thoughts on where the country is headed.

1. A short history of Brunei's monarchy, Islam and Malay identity

Brunei is the smallest country in Southeast Asia, a tiny kingdom nation-state that occupies about 6000 square kilometres with a population of around 440,000 (World Factbook 2017). It is dominated by the Malays (65.7 percent) and 78.8 percent of Brunei is Muslim (ibid.). It is "the only ASEAN[1] country that has

---

[1] ASEAN is the Association of South East Asian Nations, comprising of Brunei, Cambodia, Indonesia, Laos, Malaysia, Myanmar, the Philippines, Singapore, Thailand, and Vietnam.

unambiguously defined itself as a nonsecular 'Islamic state' since its Declaration of Independence from Britain in 1984" (Müller 2014:421). Among all Southeast Asian countries, "only in Malaysia and Brunei are 'the Malays' the majority community" (Milner 2008:1). The term describing the native people of Brunei as "Malays" has been disputed; in the nation's early history, the native inhabitants referred to themselves as "orang Brunei" or "Bruneis", rather than Malay (ibid.:13-24). This occurred during past history when many Southeast Asian sultanates "struggle[d] with one another to lead the 'Melayu' or to claim a 'Melayu' heritage" (ibid.:75).

For most of Brunei's history, "ethnic distinctions were potentially of minor significance within the indigenous population for all indigenous groups enjoyed the common status of subject of the Sultan" (Brown, cited by Milner 2008:135). Thus, the rulers discouraged 'broad-scale ethnic identities', instead preferring a classificatory 'fragmentation' of ethnic groups by local identification [to] hinder coalitions of people under them" (ibid.).

Among its other Southeast Asian neighbours (e.g. the celebrated Melaka, Pattani in southern Thailand, Sumatra and Johor), Brunei can rightly claim to be another jewel in the Malay sultanate heritage (ibid.:47). As late as "the early 1800s Brunei ... was still called ... 'the Venice of the East' and its capital ... (a 'most extraordinary town') was judged to possess "from thirty to forty thousand inhabitants" (ibid.:52). Historically, the adoption of Islam in Brunei was "presented as being led by established rulers" due to "top-down ideological leadership" (Milner 2008:43). Brunei managed to retain its distinctive identity through a powerful sultan that basically retained much of his power because in the case "of the *kerajaan* elite in Brunei ... 'there was no clear-cut distinction in the traditional value system between political and commercial functions' (Pringle, cited by Milner 2008:73).

However, when the British arrived in the northeast, "the British North Borneo Company had taken control of regions claimed either by the Brunei or the Sulu sultanate, the latter based in the southern Philippines. Brunei itself accepted a British Resident in 1906" (Milner 2008:105).

"On Borneo most of the territory of the sultan of Brunei in the northwest was appropriated by the English Brooke family, who virtually created their own *kerajaan* there" (Walker, cited by Milner

2008:105). During this time, James Brooke "introduced the category 'Malay' to Sarawak. In Sabah the British North Borneo Company used a different 'administrative vocabulary'. Muslims there continued to be called 'Brunei', 'Bajau' and so forth" (Milner 2008:121).

Even so, for most of its premodern history, colonialism did not unduly shake its monarchy. It was in the mid-twentieth century that key events unfolded that would shape Brunei's present identity. After World War II, Brunei began writing a constitution in 1959 which made provisions for elections. During this period, Brunei was invited to join independent Malaya to form Malaysia in 1963. Of all the territories in British Borneo, Brunei should perhaps have been the most enthusiastic about joining the 'Malaysia' project. A sultanate with a history intertwined in different ways with that of the Peninsular sultanates, and a majority population ... similar in culture to the 'Malays' of Malaya – although still calling themselves 'Bruneis' – the incorporation of Brunei would appear to have been a relatively easy matter (ibid.:164)

However, Brunei did not join because of anxiety that the sultan would lose powers in the Malaysian structure. Moreover, Brunei was now also aware that it had a huge oil wealth that it wanted to keep for itself. The situation was further complicated by a short-lived antimonarchical rebellion in 1962. "In 1962 the Brunei People's Party (BRP) won an overwhelming victory. During that same year, the BRP's military wing staged a revolt" (Peao 2014:24). Led by Azahari, the BRP gained popular support in the District and Legislative Council elections and had acquired something of a pan-Archipelago vision for Brunei's new modern nation-state identity. After establishing contact with Indonesian nationalists during the Japanese occupation, Azahari declared his aim in the rebellion to set up a Unitary State of North Kalimantan (using the Indonesian name for 'Borneo'). Azahari believed he was promised Indonesian military assistance but this did not materialize. His failure to persuade the traditional ruling class to set common nationalist goals led to the demise of his dream. In the year following the failed rebellion,

> the sultanate of Brunei did not become part of Malaysia. It remained under British protection and it also remained a monarchy. Sovereignty rested in the sultan, and it was his prerogative to grant a constitution. The advisory committee Sultan Omar Ali appointed in 1953 toured the state and

> visited the peninsula. Its report borrowed mainly from the Kelantan constitution, but it 'resonated with nationalistic fervour'. 'With regard to religion, inhabitants and language common in Brunei', the committee concluded, 'the policy of the Government should be that of "Islam Democracy" and the Government shall always have a sovereign Sultan who has full authority in the country (Tarling 2004:188).

Over the next decades the royal leadership of Brunei would establish a modern sultanate that became the envy of every royal family across the Archipelago – a new nation in which 'Malay' nationalism (of a type) and Islam are articulated within a *"kerajaan-*based ideology" (Milner 2008:164).

Brunei remains an absolute monarchy but it can be considered closer to a "soft form of monarchical dictatorship". The present sultan, Hassanal Bolkiah, has actually been in office since 1967, but crowned in 1968 (Kershaw, cited by Peou 2014:24) He is,

> among other things, prime minister, finance minister, and defence minister. He is also the defender of faith and a state ideology deeply rooted in Islam. The political system is based on the 1959 Constitution and ...[p]olitical power is transferred on the basis of hereditary succession (Peou 2014:25).

Elections were finally abolished in 1970 (Peao 2014:24) due to a "traumatic antimonarchical rebellion that was put down in 1962; "emergency laws, a strict legal regime, and highly powerful state institutions have been used to minimize political dissent. After five decades of systematically depoliticizing the population, there is no opposition group left, neither organized as a political party nor as civil society actors" (Müller 2016:422).

On 31 December 1983 (the same year in which Mahathir curbed the remaining powers of the Malay rulers on the peninsula), the Sultan finally proclaimed independence, and declared the state to be 'a sovereign, democratic and independent Malay Islamic Monarchy based on Islamic teachings'. MIB was announced in 1984, when the sultan declared that Brunei would

> 'forever be a Malay Islamic Monarchy." Described interchangeably as a "national philosophy," "concept of the nation," and "ideology," MIB rests on three pillars defining the core of prescribed national identity: Melayu (Malayness), Islam, and Beraja (Monarchy). In this triangle, the Islamic aspect is considered supreme. Critical scholars, none of

whom is a Bruneian citizen, have deconstructed MIB as a twentieth-century nation-building project, an "ideological construct" that has been "exploited" for self-legitimization (Müller 2016:422).

The Malay Islamic monarchy, according to the minister of religious affairs,

> "is the essence of the identity of the Brunei people and their noble Malay culture, which accepts and experiences Islam as a full and complete way of life". It presents the 'Malays' as the "dominant race" of the country, and spells out the different ways in which the government "strengthens Islam" – especially through education and preventing the promotion of other religions. But in Brunei, more than any other 'Malay' community, old kerajaan concepts continue to influence the formulation of the monarch's role. The institution of the monarch, the minister points out, provides "an identity for the Malay race", and the sovereign "holds a mandate from God". As a result of the "development of Islam" in the country, so the official philosophy insists, "the position of the monarch" will also grow even stronger (Milner 2008:223).

Melayu Islam Beraja was set out more fully as the official state philosophy on Sultan Hassanal Bolkiah's 44th birthday in 1990. In the following years it was 'elevated to its status as an ideology'. Even though the Sultan declared the state to be "'a sovereign, democratic and independent Malay Islamic Monarchy based on Islamic teachings' ... the reference to democracy in the declaration is given no institutional meaning" (Tarling 2004:189).

As one of the few countries in the world where the monarch still retains absolute power, it is the position of the Sultan as the supreme figure in MIB ideology that influences the shape, speed and sting of syariah legislation in Brunei today. However, because Islam reckons itself to be an egalitarian religion at heart, all who would claim to be chief among others potentially risk offending the guardians of its ethos (Marlow 2002).

In the past decade, Sultan Hassanal Bolkiah led his kingdom-state to implement syariah legislation with great alacrity to defuse any potential *ulama*-led criticism of the monarchy.[2] Under its MIB

---

[2] This almost echoes Malaysia's own Islamisation drive in the 1980s under then Prime Minister Dr Mahatir Mohamad. A capitalist at heart and more of a secularist, Mahathir's seeming zeal to Islamise vast swathes of the country's institutions, such as the introduction of Bank Islam, the establishment of the Islamic Centre and the International Islamic University, can be understood as

ideology, the tight linkage between the two would seal the association of the monarchy as the foremost defender and arbiter of Islam in the kingdom nation. Some think the new penal code aims to give Brunei's royals more ways to quash dissent. Another, simpler theory is that

> the sultan, who led a wild youth, has grown more religious. Zealots assert that a more pious Brunei will probably grow faster, because Allah will perhaps let it discover more hydrocarbons. The growing consensus, as one analyst puts it, is: "You don't need to work, but to pray" (*The Economist* 2015).

2. The development of syariah law in post-colonial Brunei

For the first three decades of its independence from the British since 1983, there was little demand for syariah law. However, in the past decade, "the Shariah sector was further empowered, fueled by transnational Islamic revivalism, ideological developments within Brunei's Islamic bureaucracy, power-political considerations, and the growing piety of the aging sultan, Hassanal Bokiah" (Müller 2016:426). Several factors may have contributed to this fueling of Islamic revivalism, such as recent developments of syariazation in Malaysia in the last decades (Nagata 1994), the opportunity to deflect growing economic stagnation over Brunei's recent declining oil revenues (see above), a perceived need to control non-local variants of transnational Islam such as *Darul Arqam* from spreading in the country (Abdul Hamid 2009:158) and a need to find employment for its graduates other than its already bloated public sector (Gunn 2008).

Of them all, it is likely no accident that Brunei's drive towards implementing Syariah law parallels, if not was influenced by developments in its neighbour, Malaysia, particularly in its two conservative Islamic states of Kelantan and Terengganu (see Cheong and see Yapp in this volume).

For example, in Brunei, the vast majority of departments and organizations involved in Islamic propagation and education are government-sponsored. Towards this end, the government of Brunei established the Ministry of Religious Affairs. The *Da'wah* Center under the Ministry of Religious Affairs was established for

---

attempts to bolster his weak Islamic credentials and curry the support of the rising class of Muslim intellectuals and youth of his day (Nagata 1994).

the advancement and expansion of Islam in Brunei, as well as promoting the understanding of Islam among non-Muslims in the state. Some of its activities include research on Islamic affairs, publications, exhibitions, and an archive section on Islamic civilization. In addition to producing *fatwas* (Islamic legal rulings), the Brunei State Mufti's Office provides Muslims with *irshad* (guidance) on Islamic legal matters, and is a reference center for Islamic knowledge (Yousif 2006:455).

In 2013, the *Perintah Kanun Hukuman Syariah 2013* or the Syariah Penal Code Order 2013 (henceforth SPCO) was enacted with an intent that it would be Brunei's law for the entire country. With the introduction of the SPCO, Brunei would have its own coded Islamic criminal law. In this respect it has moved ahead of Malaysia. Historically, Brunei was already ahead of the regional trend of outlawing 'deviant sects', a phenomenon that is presently causing great concern in Malaysia (*ajaran sesat*) and Indonesia (*aliran sesat*) (Müller 2016:424).

However, this placed Brunei in a particularly tricky position for in 2012 it had signed the ASEAN Human Rights Declaration (AHRD) that "expressed their commitment to religious freedom and nondiscrimination" (ibid.:415). Due to this, depending on situational contexts, Brunei's political leaders are now

> using flexible strategies to position themselves in between human rights and Shariah law. Their arguments range from the claim that human rights are essentially "Islamic" and fully compatible with Shariah law, to the accusation that human rights are Western, "man-made" inventions which are incompatible with God's legislative commandments, or must be subordinated to them. In the process of navigating between these two normative frames of reference, "human rights" is transformed into a polysemic signifier: one with multiple meanings (ibid., 416).

The AHRD also provides a backdoor by stating that "'the realisation of human rights must be considered in the regional and national context bearing in mind different political, economic, legal, social, cultural, historical and *religious* backgrounds'" [emphasis in original] (ibid., 420). It is this point that "undermines the declaration's proclaimed protection of religious freedom (ibid.), as the rest of our discussion will detail. However, we should also note that

> Brunei's Shariah legislation has long been based on a dual legal system, in which Islamic and British-derived laws coexist. Before the colonial era, the monarchy was organized under interrelated Shariah and customary law, codified as Hukum Kanun Brunei (Code of Laws of Brunei) alongside Hukum Resam and Adat Istiadat (Customary Laws). The British administration paved the way for a more systematic form of Shariah-based governance. Under Indirect Rule, British colonial advisors encouraged a "modern" codification of Islamic law and related institution building, starting in 1912 and continuing throughout the Residency period. Although most Bruneian scholars perceive colonialism as a secular or "infidel" disturbance of a previously existing "complete" Islamic order, and while colonial Shariah law was indeed largely limited to family law, the British-supported legacy of institutionalization and legalism created the foundation of today's powerful Islamic bureaucracy (ibid.:425).

Thus, what is the SPCO about? What is its impact on non-Muslims living in Brunei? In the next section, we will provide a short summary of the SPCO and briefly consider its impact on non-Muslims. We depart from an in-depth academic study of the SPCO to consider its daily influence on the nation's ordinary people, particularly Christians.

The implementation of the SPCO

Brunei's plan is to implement the SPCO in three phases. Phase One of the SPCO came into force on 1 May 2014 with provisions for offences which are punishable by fines (*Brunei Times* 2014). These offences include not fasting during Ramadan and failing to perform Friday prayers. However, the implementation of Phases Two and Three has been delayed for about two years because drafting has not yet been completed; it must be in place before the SPCO can be fully implemented (Abdullah 2014).

When Phase Two is completed, it would carry provisions such as the amputation of limbs for theft. When Phase Three is in force, the entire SPCO would be in effect, including the death penalty by stoning for adultery and rape. It is now anticipated that Phase Two will come into force in 2017 and Phase Three in 2018 (*Borneo Bulletin* 2016). Müller observes that

> Prior to 2014, Shariah law applied exclusively to Muslims, whereas non-Shariah law was applicable to all citizens. This dual system has been altered by the SPCO 2013, which

includes certain provisions for non-Muslims, including punishments such as imprisonment, and even the death penalty (e.g. for insulting Prophet Muhammad). The government has defined its new legal system as "hybrid", and claims that enforcing the SPCO 2013 will lead to a complete implementation of Islamic law (2016:426).

In its approach, Brunei has taken a different track from Malaysia in the introduction of Syariah law. While Malaysia's implementation has been more gradual and subtle, Brunei's is more direct and immediate. Certain salient aspects of the SPCO which are of relevance here will now be highlighted.

Extra territorial effect: according to Section 3(3) of the SPCO, if a resident of Brunei commits an offence in, for example Malaysia, a person could be prosecuted upon returning to Brunei. For example, the consumption of alcohol by a Muslim in Brunei is prohibited. So if a Bruneian Muslim crosses to neighbouring Malaysia and consumes alcohol there, he or she could be prosecuted upon returning to Brunei.

Application to non-Muslims: the SPCO also applies to non-Muslims. Section 3(1) expressly states that "Except as otherwise expressly provided therein, this Order applies to Muslims and non-Muslims". Consequently, if a non-Muslim steals, his hand could also be cut off. Under Section 63(1)(b)(i) of the SPCO the punishment for a first offence of theft is the amputation of the right hand from the wrist joint. For a second offence, the punishment is amputation of the left foot up to the ankle. For the third and subsequent offence, the punishment is imprisonment not exceeding fifteen years. As the SPCO will co-exist with Brunei's civil law Penal Code, it remains to be seen how this co-existence will work in practice. If a non-Muslim is charged with theft, will the offender be prosecuted under the SPCO or the civil law Penal Code (which does not carry the punishment of amputation of limbs)? Another example is if any non-Muslim commits adultery with a Muslim, the former could be punished by being stoned to death [Section 69(3) of the SPCO]. But if it is adultery between two non-Muslims, only then are they not punishable under the SPCO.

In another example, under Sections 104(5) and (6) of the SPCO, a non-Muslim who drinks in public or gives a gift of liquor to a Muslim friend is liable to a fine not exceeding BN$8,000, imprisonment not exceeding 2 years or both. In this respect, compared to Malaysia's current design of its syariah law, Brunei's version does not differentiate between a Muslim versus a non-Muslim – both fall under its jurisdiction.

<u>Restrictions on proselytization</u>: the SPCO also affects and restricts proselytization. We will briefly look at some relevant provisions.

Apostasy carries very serious consequences in Brunei. Any Muslim who declares himself a non-Muslim, if convicted, is punishable by death [Section 112(1) of the SPCO]. A person who abets or aids in the commission of apostasy is liable to imprisonment of up to thirty years and whipping not exceeding forty strokes [Section 114 of the SPCO]. Furthermore under Section 209(1) of the SPCO, propagation of a religion other than Islam to a Muslim or to a person having no religion is an offence punishable by a fine not exceeding BN$20,000, imprisonment not exceeding five years or both. A person who persuades, tells, influences, incites, encourages or lets a Muslim to become a believer or member of a religion other than Islam or to become inclined to that religion is punishable by a fine not exceeding BN$20,000 and imprisonment not exceeding five years [Section 210(1) of the SPCO]. This section is very broad in its scope as it is targeted at persons who "persuades, tells, influences, incites, encourages".

The law is so broad that it even covers non-Muslims. A person who persuades or influences a person having no religion to become a believer or member of a religion other than Islam or to become inclined to that religion or to dislike the religion of Islam is punishable by a fine not exceeding BN$20,000 and imprisonment not exceeding five years [Section 211(a) and (b) of the SPCO]. This Section thus extends the prohibition on proselytisation to persons who have no religion. Arguably animists could be considered to be persons who have no religion as well as atheists.

Any person who persuades, tells, causes, influences, incites, encourages or lets a Muslim child or a child whose parents have no religion who is under eighteen years (i) to accept the teachings of a religion other than Islam (ii) to attend any ceremony, act of worship or religious activities of any religion other than Islam (iii) to participate in any activities held for the benefit of any religion other than Islam, is punishable by a fine not exceeding BN$20,000 and imprisonment not exceeding five years [Section 212(a), (b) and (c) of the SPCO].

Here, it is difficult to fathom the apparent reason that Brunei would prohibit proselytisation towards a group of people that are non-

Muslims. However some people in Brunei privately expressed the view that this law seemed to be designed to prevent any Christian missionising of the indigenous non-Malays of Brunei, such as the Ibans or Kenyah (who are animists) who resided there, and pave the way for Muslims to convert them into Islam.

Here, we note that in Brunei, Christians only number around 9 percent (*World Factbook* 2017). The Anglican and Roman Catholic Church has two churches in Bandar Seri Begawan (Brunei's capital), Kota Beliat and Seria. Where any other Christians or churches exist in Brunei, they are likely unregistered or unofficial churches that officials may know of but choose to overlook unless they overtly intrude on some Muslim sensitivity, such as disturbing the peace by overcrowding a parking space normally reserved for commercial shop lots, or offending a local government official.[3]

However, in light of these sections in the SPCO, interactions between Christians and Muslims will have to be more circumspect and consider these wide-ranging prohibitions especially when a conversation strays into areas concerning non-Islamic religions.

Prohibitions on mocking Islam: the SPCO also contains prohibitions on mocking and ridiculing Islam.

In Section 217 of the SPCO, a non-Muslim who uses certain specific words (eg. Allah, al-Qur'an, *azan, hadith, haji, mufti*) in a publication or speech to state or express any fact, belief, idea, concept, act or activity relating to a religion other than Islam is punishable by up to BN$12,000, up to three years in prison, or both. In addition, a non-Muslim who orally, in writing or visible representation, brings into contempt, insults, makes fun of, mocks, mimics or ridicules the teaching of Islam, the practice or ceremony related to Islam, words regarded as holy by Muslims, any law in force related to Islam is punishable by up to BN$12,000, up to three years in prison, or both (Section 220 of the SPCO). Under Section 221(2), a non-Muslim "who orally, in writing, by visible representation or in any other manner ... brings into contempt Nabi Muhammad" is punishable by death. A non-Muslim who derides, mocks, mimics, ridicules by word or deed any verse of the al-Qur'an or hadith is punishable by death (Section 222(1) of the SPCO).

---

[3] With such a small number of Christians amongst the overwhelming Malay Muslim populace, it is remarkable that the government would be troubled to such an extent.

All of these laws are not only similar to, but go further than Malaysia; the main difference being that the larger presence of non-Muslims (over 35 percent) in Malaysia's population and its dual legal system makes mimicking Brunei's law politically and legally difficult for its Muslim religious authorities.

3. Brunei's Syariah law and its impact on daily living

Law, as it is codified, is only as effective as the power that state authorities confer upon its agents to enforce it, the frequency of its enforcement, the decisiveness of its punishment and pressures created by members of its society to make ordinary citizens abide or ignore it altogether. Here, we ask, what real impact, if any, does Brunei's syariah law have on its people, in particular Christians, on a day-to-day basis?

At the outset when the introduction of the SPCO was announced, there was widespread concern among non-Muslims. However, now that Phase One has been introduced and Phase Two is imminent, there is an air of resignation due to the absolute power that Sultan Hassanal Bolkiah holds and the lack of any democratic system or powerful counter that can challenge its implementation. People have largely adopted a wait-and-see attitude to see how far the state will go with the SPCO.

At the ground level, certain new measures have been imposed in recent years which have affected its residents. An example relates to Ramadan. Restaurants and food shops cannot serve dine-in customers during fasting hours. No eating is allowed in public, therefore customers can only order takeaway food during the fasting hours of the day. Even Chinese shops selling non-halal meals are included, despite an absence of Muslim clientele! This has forced all Chinese food operators to follow the law lest they, according to one resident, "tempt Muslims who are weak when they pass by the shops and smell the food". As for alcohol, it is banned. However, a non-Muslim may purchase it outside of Brunei and bring it back; upon arrival at the customs check, they must declare the quantity they are bringing in (limited to one bottle of wine and/or 6-packs of beer) and it must only be for personal consumption. Failure to declare has led to the confiscation of such controlled items.

On Friday, all Bruneian Muslims are legally obligated to fulfill their *Jumaat* prayers. Failing to do so is a criminal offense (Section 194 of the SPCO). Related to this, all shops and offices (including those run by non-Muslims) are now required to close from 12-2pm on

Fridays so that Muslims can attend to their religious duties undisturbed nor tempted by thought of business transactions.

In the education sector, all female students, including non-Muslims, are required to wear the *tudung*, i.e., a large Malay Muslim veil that covers the head to the upper body. Islamic studies has also been introduced for all students from primary school age to university level. The sole exception is at international schools. However, unless non-Muslims are wealthy, sending their children to Brunei's international schools is difficult. Needless to say, this has caused great concern amongst Christian parents.

One particular provision of the law drew widespread ridicule and scorn: the public dissemination of beliefs or practices that are considered contrary to Islamic law, or exposing Muslims to ceremonies, acts or doctrines that contradict Islamic law, which is punishable by up to five years in prison (Müller 2016:427). This led to the banned display of any Christmas trees and decorations, playing of carols, whether in hotels, malls, shops or restaurants in public. When Christians desire to do any of the above, it is now restricted to the confines of their church compound or house; even then, these displays must not be visible from a public street! According to Sultan Hassanal Bolkiah, it could "damage the faith of Muslims" (Henderson 2015).

Few Bruneians doubt that the SPCO will be fully in force by 2018. However, when this occurs, will the authorities enforce certain punishments to the fullest extent such as the amputation of limbs or death by stoning? Or will there be an element of moderation in its enforcement? Müller (2016:428) comments that

> several of these offenses were also forbidden before the legal reform. However, the punishments have been drastically increased, and additional provisions have been added. The government strongly emphasizes the procedural principle of doubt on the part of the accused, which makes it difficult to convict persons who refuse to make voluntary confessions, and various mechanisms for repentance and the lifting of sentences. It remains to be seen how the SPCO will finally be enacted in practice.

Lastly, it is difficult to see how the SPCO can be effectively implemented in its extra territorial applications. The effectiveness of this aspect of the SPCO will likely be limited as prosecutions will hinge on the availability of eyewitnesses who are prepared to give testimony on the conduct of the accused while overseas.

4. Implications for the church in Brunei

Due to the SPCO's harsh penalties, the non-negotiable process of its implementation, and the all-encompassing scope that places even non-Muslims under the same legal jurisdiction and punishments in many of its stipulations, there seems little that the Church can do except pray and hope for the best.

In Malaysia, when the Islamic authorities attempted to accelerate and implement syariah law via various political means, the presence of independent, moderate Malay Muslim voices, a strong civil society that included NGOs and a somewhat functional legislative and judiciary system, all worked to moderate and sometimes forestall various attempts. However, "unlike in Malaysia, no politician or social actor has ever publicly suggested or demanded that Brunei be 'secular' nor openly opposed the Sultan's directives (Müller 2016:425).

In contrast to other Muslim-majority countries, Brunei's Islamic policies "are discussed internally and . . . introduced slowly and quietly. Open religious polemics and debates have never taken place." (Mansurnoor, cited by Müller 2016:424).

Optimistically, the SPCO does impact local Christians in many ways, but an informant states that it is "not yet too significant". Even so, though Brunei may be small, its syariah legislation and effect on the non-Muslim citizens of its country are important to track as Sultan Hassanal Bolkiah has expressed his hope that Brunei's SPCO 2013 would become an "example for the rest of Southeast Asia" to emulate (Müller 2016:437). This was clearly evident when

> Malaysian politicians and *ulama* ... described Brunei as a role model, and discussed how a similar reform could be realized in Malaysia. In December 2013 the sultan of the PAS-controlled Malaysian state of Kelantan made an official visit to Brunei, followed soon after by Kelantan's chief minister and a state government delegation. [They all] unanimously emphasised their admiration of Brunei's "courage" and declared their intention to "learn" from its Shariah legislation. Shortly afterward, a delegation from the Malaysian state of Selangor's Fatwa Committee visited Brunei (ibid.:437-438).

Most recently, a delegation headed by Malaysia's Ministry of Religious Affairs visited Brunei in September 2014 to learn about "the implementation of various Islamic initiatives, which include the Syariah Penal Code Order 2013" (ibid.:438).

Not surprisingly, "encouraged by the Brunei-inspired wave of intensified pro-hudud sentiment, the Kelantan legislative assembly passed its own hudud act in March 2015, notably also planning on implementation in "stages" (ibid.:439). As we have seen in this volume, how much Kelantan may succeed in obtaining national sanction and authority to enforce it will certainly influence Malaysia's syariah laws in the future.

However, Brunei's syariazation process has not proceeded without its hiccups. At the time of writing, it is still stuck in Phase Two of its implementation and there are no signs of it proceeding onward to its more draconian stage. There are concerns among Brunei's Islamic authorities that not all of its officers, particularly the police officers and many senior officers who are Western-educated, have supported it. In January 2016, the Sultan even sharply criticized the Ministry of Religious Affairs for not having finalized the Syariah criminal code yet (Müller 2016:426) and directly questioned the government over their apparent foot-dragging over the process of its implementation (Borneo Bulletin 2016).

This is ironic because Brunei has been unhindered due to a lack of any independent authority that can oppose the Sultan. Yet, against such a seeming monopoly of power, the state's hesitancy and slow-footedness of its officers to do so tells a different story than the official version. However, its stalled progress does not mean it has halted from proceeding onward. Unless some extraordinary or unpredictable event occurs, the shadow that Brunei's syariah law casts over the Church will not only likely hinder its own Christians in the near foreseeable future, it may well also foreshadow other developments in Southeast Asia.

References

Abdul Hamid, Ahmad Fauzi. 2009. Transnational Islam in Malaysia. In *Transnational Islam in South and Southeast Asia: Movements, Networks, and Conflict Dynamics*, NBR Project Report April 2009. Seattle, WA: The National Bureau of Asian Research.

Abdullah, Ayla. 2014. Brunei Syariah Penal Code Order 2013: An Overview. *BSP LGL*, 15 May 2014.

Brunei Times. 2014. Implementation of Syariah law. 15 December. https://btarchive.org/news/national/2014/12/15/implementation-syariah-law (accessed 13 June 2017).

Borneo Bulletin. 2016. His Majesty lambasts delay in Syariah law enforcement. February 28. http://borneobulletin.com.bn/his-majesty-lambasts-delay-in-syariah-law-enforcement/ (accessed 12 June 2017).

Gunn, Geoffrey C. 2008. Trophy Capitalism,' Jefrinomics, and Dynastic Travail in Brunei. *The Asia-Pacific Journal*. 6, no.3. http://apjjf.org/-Geoffrey-Gunn/2696/article.html (accessed 12 June 2017).

Henderson, Barney. 2015. Sultan of Brunei bans Christmas because it could damage the faith of Muslims. *The Telegraph* 22 December. http://www.telegraph.co.uk/topics/christmas/12063373/Sultan-of-Brunei-bans-Christmas-because-it-could-damage-faith-of-Muslims.html (accessed 26 December 2015).

Milner, Anthony. *The Malays*. Malden, MA: Wiley-Blackwell.

Morris, Regan. 2014. Stars boycott Beverly Hills Hotel over Brunei 'sharia'. *BBC News*. 7 May. http://www.bbc.com/news/world-us-canada-27303085 (accessed 9 June 2017).

Müller, Dominik. 2016. Paradoxical normalities in Brunei and Malaysia. *Asian Survey* 56, no.3: 415-441.

Nagata, Judith. 1994. How to be Islamic without being an Islamic state. In *Islam, globalization and postmodernity*, ed. Akbar S. Ahmed and Donnan Hastings, 63-90. New York: Routledge.

Peou, Sorpong. 2014. The limits and potential of liberal democratisation in Southeast Asia. *Journal of Current Southeast Asian Affairs* 33, no.3:19–47.

Syariah Penal Code Order. 2013. http://www.agc.gov.bn/AGC%20Images/LAWS/Gazette_PDF/2013/EN/syariah%20penal%20code%20order 2013.pdf (accessed 12 June 2017).

Tarling, Nicholas 2004. *Nationalism in Southeast Asia*. New York: RoutledgeCurzon.

The Economist. 2014. All pray and no work: An autocratic sultanate turns more devout as oil money declines. 15 August. http://www.economist.com/news/asia/21661040-autocratic-sultanate-turns-more-devout-oil-money-declines-all-pray-and-no-work? Fsrc=rss (accessed 13 December 2015).

Yousif. Ahmad F. 2006. Contemporary Islamic movements in Southeast Asia: Challenges and opportunities. In *The Blackwell companion to contemporary Islamic thought*, ed. Ibrahim M. Abu-Rabi', 449-465. New York: Wiley-Blackwell.

World Factbook. 2017. Brunei. https://www.cia.gov/library/publications/the-world-factbook/geos/bx.html (accessed 7 June 2017).

Part B

Case Studies of the Church under the Shadow of Shariah in Malaysia

The Church under the Shadow of Shariah: Exploring Dimension and Responses in Malaysia

Eugene Yapp

The Islamic bureaucracy in Malaysia is once again asserting that the country is an Islamic state and therefore warrants the implementation of Shariah in the areas of policy, law and politics. This assertion can be traced back to former Prime Minister Datuk Seri Dr Mahathir Mohamad's opening address at the Gerakan Party's 30th national delegates' conference on 29 September 2001:

> UMNO wishes to state loudly that Malaysia is an Islamic country. This is based on the opinion of ulamaks who had clarified what constituted as [sic] Islamic country. If Malaysia is not an Islamic country because it does not implement the hudud, then there are no Islamic countries in the world. If UMNO says that Malaysia is an Islamic country, it is because in an Islamic country non-Muslims have specific rights. This is in line with the teachings of Islam.[1]

Wanting to expand this line of thought, in Parliament on 17 June 2002, Mahathir subsequently stated that Malaysia is an <u>Islamic fundamentalist</u> country.[2] The thrust of Mahathir's declarations in 2001 and 2002 created a lasting impression in the minds of many Muslims that Malaysia is indeed an Islamic State and that Islamic law ought to find its proper place in the Malaysian legal and social order. Recent judicial cases appear to have confirmed this thrust; that Shariah or Islamic law must now take centre stage in the administration of justice in Malaysian society.

Given this scenario, the theme of this volume is a timely one. It adequately expresses the silent or unspoken sentiments within the Malaysian Christian community that the country's secular legal and

---

[1] https://www.malaysiakini.com, 29th September 2001
[2] https://www.malaysiakini.com/news/11804

social order is indeed giving way to the increasing dominance of Shariah or Islamic laws. For the church to formulate a strategic response, it is necessary to undertake a study on the nature of Shariah, the content of the Islamic legislation, and its implications for Malaysian society. This essay will conclude by considering some critical issues that shape the responses of the church. It is our hope that this reading will encourage a conversation on what it means to be a witness for Christ in this age of growing religious radicalisation in Malaysia.

Is Shariah Part of Malaysian Law?

Article 3 of the Federal Constitution of Malaysia states that Islam is the religion of the Federation, while also allowing for the peaceful practice of other religions. While Islam is declared as the religion of the Federation of Malaysia, this does not mean that Malaysia is understood as an Islamic State.[3] The Constitutional Commission of the Federation of Malaya (Reid Commission) reiterated that Article 3 did not affect Malaya's position as a secular state.[4]

This was also the position when the Federation of Malaysia was formed in 1963 with the coming together of Malaya with Singapore, North Borneo (now Sabah) and Sarawak. The Cobbold Commission and Inter-governmental Commission recorded that there was opposition in North Borneo and Sarawak to making Islam the official religion of Malaysia, to which the Federal Government responded that Malaysia would remain a secular nation. Islam was to be the religion of the federation for official purposes only.[5]

Despite this declaration, the constitution of Malaysia does provide for the practice of Shariah and the establishment of Shariah courts in limited areas of Muslim belief and practice. In the Nine Schedule, Legislative List, List II-State List of the Federal Constitution of Malaysia, it is specifically provided,

> Except with respect to the Federal Territories of Kuala Lumpur and Labuan, Islamic law and personal and family law of persons professing the religion of Islam, including the Islamic law relating to succession, testate and intestate,

---

[3] Ahmad Ibrahim, "The position of Islam in the Constitution of Malaysia", in A. Ibrahim, S. Siddique and Y. Hussain (eds.), *Readings on Islam in Southeast Asia* (Singapore, Institute of Southeast Asian Studies), 1985

[4] Report of the Federation of Malaysia Constitutional Commission, para 168, 100

[5] Cobbold Report 'Recommendations' Section A para 148 (e)

> betrothal, marriage, divorce, dower, maintenance, adoption, legitimacy guardianship, gifts, partitions and non- charitable trusts; Wakafs and the definition and regulation of charitable and religious endowments, institutions, trusts, charities and charitable institutions operating wholly within the State; Malay customs. Zakat, Fitrah and Baitulmal or similar Islamic religious revenue, mosques or any Islamic public places of worship ...

The same schedule also establishes the jurisdiction of the Shariah courts as follows,

> The constitution, organisation and procedure of Syariah courts, which shall have jurisdiction only over person [sic] professing the religion of Islam and in respect only of any of the matters included in this paragraph, but shall not have jurisdiction in respect of offences except in so far as conferred by federal law ...

Shad Saleem Faruqi, Emeritus Professor of Law at Universiti Teknologi Mara, opined that

> "there are twenty four civil matters and one criminal matter, that is, 'creation and punishment of offences by persons professing the religion of Islam against precepts of that religion' in this list.[6]

In this list, it is clear that Shariah was intended for limited application only in matters of personal faith, family law and the religious practice of Muslims. Likewise, the Shariah courts' jurisdiction is only over these matters. These rulings do not allow for Shariah to act as basic law; i.e. the foundation upon which all other laws or policies are to be formulated and implemented.

Today, Article 3 has been re-interpreted in what is known as the 'silent re-writing of the Constitution' to create a legal system where Islamic law is to be the basic law of the land with civil laws being subordinate to it. Islam as the "official" religion of the Federation must now be protected and defended when under threat.[7] This has resulted in greater polarisation and restriction in religious freedom

---

[6] http://www.thestar.com.my/opinion/columnists/reflecting-on-the-law/2016/06/09/enhancing-syariah-courts-powers-the-syariah-courts-criminal-jurisdiction-act-1965-reignites-some-cri/. Accessed on 20 September 2016

[7] See the case of Menteri Dalam Negeri & Anor v Titular Roman Catholic Archbishop of Kuala Lumpur [2013] 8 CLJ 890

for both Muslims and non-Muslims following a state version of Islam which has distinctly *salafi-wahhabi* resemblances.[8]

The Empowerment of the Shariah Courts

In 1988, Parliament amended the Federal Constitution of Malaysia to provide that civil courts shall have no jurisdiction over matters relating to Shariah law.[9] The intention as expressed by then Prime Minister Dr Mahathir was,

> One thing that has brought about dissatisfaction among the Islamic community in this country is the situation whereby any civil court is able to change or cancel a decision made by the Shariah court ... The government feels that a situation like this affects the sovereignty of the Shariah court and the execution of Shariah law among the Muslims of this country. It is very important to secure the sovereignty of the Shariah court to decide on matters involving its jurisdiction, what more [sic] if the matter involves Shariah law ...[10]

While the intention may have been to prevent Muslims from evading decisions of Shariah courts by seeking recourse in the civil courts, some people argue that it is in the Government's interest to safeguard and secure the sovereignty of the Shariah courts. Over time, the sovereignty of the Shariah court has been given concrete expression when civil Muslim judges began declining involvement in cases when one party is a Muslim, thereby ceding jurisdiction on issues of fundamental liberties to the Shariah courts. The intention to alleviate and expand the jurisdiction of the Shariah courts is clearly on the Government's agenda.[11]

The Shariah Legislation

Moh'd Hashim Kamali defined Shariah as that which "pertains to or closely identifies with divine revelation, the knowledge of which could only be obtained from the Quran and Sunna".[12] It literally means the "path to the watering-place, the clear path to be followed and the path which the believer has to tread in order to obtain

---

[8] M.N. Osman, 'Towards a History of Malaysian Ulama', *Working papers*, S. Rajaratnam School of International Studies (2007)

[9] Article 121(1)(A) Federal Constitution of Malaysia

[10] Minutes of the *Dewan Rakyat*, 17 March 1988, section 1364

[11] See http://www.themalaymailonline.com/malaysia/article/jakim-confirms-putrajayas-plan-for-shariah-equivalent-to-federal-court

[12] Mohammad Hashim Kamali, *Shari'ah Law: An Introduction*. (Oxford: Oneworld Publications), 2008, 14

guidance in this world and deliverance in the next".[13] In popular understanding, Shariah refers to the "commands, prohibitions, guidance and principles that God has addressed to mankind pertaining to their conduct in this world and salvation in the next".[14]

Thus man is to follow the precepts of Shariah in order to ascertain the will of the divine and to establish the good and justice in accordance with Shariah, the divine way. Shariah is therefore correlated with 'following' (*din*) in that Muslims are enjoined to follow the divinely ordained 'way-to-be-followed' (Q.45:18).[15] Shariah is therefore revealed in the Qur'an and Sunna and contains legal rulings and broad principles that have moral and spiritual import. These broad principles and legal rulings have been later interpreted and applied to concrete situations of human life through understanding (*fiqh*) of the legal jurists. Over time, the interpretations and understandings together with their distinctive methodologies formed a particular school of law.[16] Shariah is therefore an essential component of the Muslim faith, an indispensable part of the religion. Norani Othman points out,

> Shariah is indeed a central concern in the private and public life of a majority of contemporary Muslims. It has a paramount role in the public life of Islamic societies, for it provides the main reference for shaping and developing ethical norms and values that are the basis of public law and public policy in many Muslim countries, such as Saudi Arabia, Pakistan and Malaysia.[17]

In Malaysia, the dominant school of Shariah is the Sunni Shafi'i school of thought, although the views and opinions of other established schools are acceptable. A main feature of the administration of Islam in the country is legislation in the form of

---

[13] *Ibid.*

[14] *Ibid.*

[15] Fazlur Rahman, *Islam*, 2nd ed. (Chicago: Chicago University Press), 2002, 100

[16] See Mashood A. Baderin, Administration of Justice under the Shari'ah, Common Law and Civil Law System: Towards a Better Understanding, Vol 2 *Malaysian Journal of Syariah and Law* (2010), 1-48. Baderin listed the following methods and principles in the application of laws such as *darurah* (necessity), *maslahah* (welfare), *istihsan* (equity), *takhayur* (eclectic choice), *talfiq* (patching up), *siyasah sharliyyah* (politics) and *maqasid al-sharilah* (the higher objective of law)

[17] Norani Othman, "Islam, Constitution, Citizenship Rights and Justice in Malaysia", in Birgit Krawietz and Helmut Reifeld (eds.), *Islam and the Rule of Law: Between Sharia and Secularization* (Berlin, Germany: *Konrad-Adenauer-Stiftung e.V*), 2008

Islamic enactments, which contain the legal rulings and broad principles of Shariah. These enactments are administered and given coercive force by a sophisticated Islamic bureaucracy and institutions that form part of the state apparatus.[18]

The genesis of these Islamic enactments began with the Pangkor Treaty of 1874 whereby the British established a system of rule allowing the Malay rulers to oversee matters of religion and custom (*adat*), while English law was to govern all other aspects of commercial and civic life. To assist the Malay rulers in this task, the British instituted a Muhammadian Marriage Enactment in 1880 (to regulate Muslim family law in the Straits Settlements), and courts were established with jurisdiction over Muslim family law matters.[19] In due course, similar Muhammadian marriage and divorce enactments followed in all the other States in the colony.[20]

In 1952, a second set of Muslim enactments followed, including the Administration of Muslim Law Enactment of Selangor. The Selangor enactment was essentially positive law styled in a legal code that delineated certain aspects of Shariah that applied to Muslims. The enactment detailed the membership, functions and powers of a Majlis Ugama Islam dan Adat Istiadat Melayu (Council of Religion and Malay Custom); including regulations concerning marriage, divorce and criminal offences; and the functions and procedures of the religious courts.[21] The Selangor enactment also provided a template for other states to follow.[22]

---

[18] An example is the formation of a National Council for Islamic Affairs (Pusat Islam) that was administered by the Department of Religion (Jabatan Agama) under the Prime Minister's Department. Later, the Jabatan Agama was reorganized and renamed as the Jabatan Kemajuan Islam Malaysia, better known as JAKIM. It has been reported that JAKIM has a budget allocation by the state amounting to RM1 billion for its activities and operations. This budget allocation has been called into question by the public and even by the Malay rulers themselves. See http://www.themalaymailonline.com/malaysia/article/johor-sultan-why-does-jakim-need-rm1b-budget

[19] Donald L. Horowitz, The Qur'an and the Common Law: Islamic Law Reform and the Theory of Legal Change, 42 *American Journal of Comparative Law* (1994) 543-580

[20] For the State of Perak in 1885, the State of Kedah in 1919, the State of Kelantan in 1915.

[21] Tamir Moustafa, Judging in God's Name: State Power, Secularism, and the Politics of Islamic law in Malaysia, *Oxford Journal of Law and Religion* (2013), 1–16

[22] *Ibid.* For the State of Terengganu in 1955, the State of Pahang in 1956, the State of Malacca in 1959, the State of Penang in 1959, the State of Negeri Sembilan in 1960, the State of Kedah in 1962, the State of Perlis in 1964 and the State of Perak in 1965

Present day Islamic enactments containing substantive laws may be divided into three categories as follows:[23]

- Laws on the Administration of Islam

    This is the principal law enacted by the various States within the Federation of Malaysia to administer and regulate the affairs of Islam as empowered by List II-State List such as the creation of a Majlis Agama (Islamic Council), Jabatan Agama (Islamic Department), constitution and powers of the Shariah courts, the giving of fatwas, and on matters such as conversion to Islam and other related matters.

- Islamic Family Law

    This is the law that administers and regulates Islamic family matters such as the institution of marriage; the act and grounds of divorce; subsequent questions of child custody; maintenance of family members; inheritance; among others.

- Laws on Shariah Criminal Offences

    This is the law that stipulates the nature of the various offences in Islam and the appropriateness of their respective punishments. Examples include the offence of intoxication; *khalwat* (close proximity); and refusal to fast or being caught not fasting during the month of Ramadan.

These Islamic enactments regulate the affairs and conduct of Muslims in their state localities.[24] Debates and discussions continue as to whether these Islamic enactments consistently represent what Shariah is or ought to be. There is also the problem of uniformity of position and opinion in terms of the administration, regulation and enforcement of Islamic laws in the different States. This diversity of opinion has often led to confusion and uncertainty in Islamic legislation.[25]

---

[23] These are merely substantive enactments. In addition to the substantive enactments, there are also procedural enactments that deal with due processes of the shari'ah courts and evidential enactments that detailed means of evidence and procedures, which will not be discussed here in this essay.

[24] For references to these Islamic enactments, see Appendix One

[25] For example, the Institute of Islamic Understanding (IKIM), has recognised that the non-uniformity in Islamic law has led to apparent disunity among Muslims, followed by

More recently, Tamir Moustafa raised a fundamental question whether these Islamic enactments in their substantive form truly represent Shariah. He asserts that these Islamic enactments are in reality characterized by a "peculiar mix of legal traditions". He continues:

> The law was 'Anglo' in the sense that the concepts, categories, and modes of analysis followed English common law, and it was 'Muslim' in the sense that it contained fragments of Islamic jurisprudence that were applied to Muslim subjects. As such, Anglo-Muslim law was an entirely different creature from classical Islamic law.[26]

Although his conclusion will likely be challenged by the State religious authorities, his arguments have not been addressed and left largely unanswered. We may therefore make two salient observations here.

Firstly, if indeed these Islamic enactments contain fragments of Islamic jurisprudence, it would mean they represent mere human expression and conception rather than the divinely-guided way as claimed in classical Shariah. If the laws are human legislation, they must certainly be open to challenge as to their validity or legal application like any other laws of the land.

Secondly, if the objective of Shariah is justice, would these Islamic enactments couched in human categories really bring justice for all Muslims everywhere and in every situation? This is a critical question that ought to be answered if the enactments are to gain widespread public acceptance and credibility amongst the various religious communities in the country. It remains to be seen if this is really the case.

Impact on the Church

Notwithstanding that Shariah is part of the Malaysian legal system in areas of personal law and belief, freedom of religion for all religious communities is preserved under the Malaysian Constitution. But there are now certain quarters who argue that Islam and the wider interest of the Muslim community must take

---

misperception among the non-Muslims, leaving them both perplexed and confused. See http://www.ikim.gov.my/index.php/en/the-star/7480-non-uniformity-of-islamic-law

[26] Moustafa, Judging in God's Name, 9

precedence over the right of freedom of religion and that the State or its institution is obliged to protect the position of Islam.[27]

Such an assertion would only confirm the fears of the church that Shariah or Islamic law would eventually take the place as the dominant law of the land overriding civil law. The fears are not unfounded and may be illustrated clearly in three areas of public contestation; conflicts of laws and jurisdiction, the enforcement of the *hudud* laws and expanding the powers of the Shariah courts.

Conflict of Laws and Jurisdiction

In a situation where one spouse in a non-Muslim marriage converts to Islam and at the same time converts the children to Islam without the knowledge or consent of the non-Muslim spouse, the non-Muslim spouse would have no avenue to challenge the children's conversion to Islam. This is a given, as civil courts have decided that any matters relating to conversion to Islam fall under the jurisdiction of Shariah courts and can no longer be heard by the civil courts. This presents a dilemma for the non-Muslim parent who now cannot appear either in the civil or Shariah court simply because the Shariah courts have no jurisdiction over non-Muslims.[28]

This situation would be further complicated if similar custody orders were issued by both the civil court and Shariah court over the same children. Indeed, in a real life example of this situation, the police refused to enforce a court order to assist in locating and returning a child taken forcibly by the converting Muslim parent from the non-Muslim parent. This was on the grounds that there are two conflicting custody orders from *courts of competing jurisdiction.*[29]

The problems and difficulties with divorce and custody cases have become increasingly apparent due to the conflict of civil and Shariah laws and the dual jurisdiction between the Shariah courts and the civil courts. These contradictions of law and jurisdiction

---

[27] See the judgement of Justice Dato Sri Haji Mohamed Apandi Bin Haji Ali (as he then was) in Menteri Dalam Negeri & Ors v Titular Roman Catholic Archbishop of Kuala Lumpur (2013) MLJU 1060 (Court of Appeal judgment)

[28] As in the case of Viran a/l Nagapan v Deepa a/p Subramaniam (Peguam Negara & Anor, Intervener) [2015] 3 MLJ 209; and Pathmanathan a/l Krishnan v Indira Gandhi a/p Mutho. Civil Appeal No. A-02-1826-08 [2013] (Court of Appeal)

[29] In the case of Pathmanathan a/l Krishnan v Indira Gandhi a/p Mutho, the Inspector General of Police, himself a Muslim, stated publicly that he could be in contempt of the shari'ah court if he enforced the civil court order to locate and return the child. See report at http://www.themalaymailonline.com/malaysia/article/impossible-to-comply-with-order-to-retrieve-indiras-child-igps-lawyer-tells

have not been resolved *in toto* with the present outcome leading to greater suspicion and anxiety amongst non-Muslim communities.

Enforcement of the Hudud Laws

In 1993, the State of Kelantan passed the Kelantan Syariah Criminal Code (II) Enactment 1993 which seeks to provide and enforce specific punishments laid down by the Qur'an and Hadith as part of the penal legal system. The Kelantan Syariah Criminal Code was amended in 2015 with slight variation in terms of punishments. Since then, this criminal code has come to be popularly known as the "*hudud* laws".

Following the State of Kelantan, the State of Terengganu also passed the Terengganu Syariah Criminal Offense (Hudud and Qisas) Enactment of 2003. Its provisions and punishments by and large follow the provisions of the Kelantan Syariah Criminal Code.

When the Kelantan Syariah Criminal Code bill was first introduced, grave concerns were expressed by both the non-Muslim communities and the Federal government. The Federal government, then under Mahathir's administration, was not keen to have hudud laws introduced to the legal system as they deemed the civil criminal law code as sufficient. As events transpired, the Federal government did not support the bill and with Parliament refusing to authorise the State Legislature to make such laws, the bill, though passed by the State Legislature, became unconstitutional.[30]

There are two areas of major concern for non-Muslims in regards to the hudud laws. Firstly, although the Kelantan state government declares the law will only apply to Muslims, non-Muslims may choose to have the law apply to them too.[31] This demonstrates that the hudud law is not exclusive to Muslims only. This enactment leaves open the possibility in the future that the law may apply to non-Muslims. At present there are already calls by certain Muslims or traditionalist groups to make the law applicable to all..[32]

---

[30] This is by virtue of Article 76A(1) of the Federal Constitution which provides for Parliament to authorise the Legislatures of the States, subject to such conditions or restrictions as parliament may impose, to make laws with respect to criminal law matters which are under the jurisdiction of Parliament. For the hudud bills, that did not happen.

[31] This was in the original provision. In the recent amendment to the bill, this provision was removed.

[32] See report at http://www.themalaymailonline.com/malaysia/article/dont-exempt-non-muslims-from-hudud-muslim-scholars-suggest

Secondly, Muslim jurists have understood the objective of the *hadd* penalties as protecting public interest. They are therefore labelled as claims of God (*huquq Allah*) and not claims of men; rendering their sentences as fixed by God and immutable.[33] As the laws are for public interest, there are stringent requirements for conviction and a strict evidential burden to fulfil. Rudolph Peters summarised the difficulties in obtaining a conviction through "(1) the strict rules of evidence for proving these crimes; (2) the extensive opportunities to use the notion of uncertainty (*shubha*) as a defence; and (3) defining the crime very strictly, so that many similar acts fall outside the definition and cannot be punished with fixed penalties, but only at discretion".[34]

The question is whether the hudud laws, if enforced, afford the same latitude and same burden of proof consistent with classical Islamic jurisprudence. There is an absence of discussion on such details and means of enforcement. There is also a lack of clarity on issues of methodology and application. The concern of the church is that such laws will only lead to greater injustice and abuse of the law.

Expanding Powers of the Shariah Courts

On 26 May 2016, a Private Member's Bill was tabled as motion for debate in the Dewan Rakyat (Lower House of the Malaysian Parliament). The subject matter was the Shariah Courts (Criminal Jurisdiction) (Amendment) Bill 2016. According to reports, the bill was aimed at upgrading the jurisdiction of the Shariah courts and does not cover non-Muslims.[35]

Not unexpectedly, the Bill and the manner by which it was tabled in Parliament received due criticism from all quarters.[36] Notwithstanding the government's assurance that the purpose of the Bill is not about implementing the hudud laws or an attempt in "backdoor Islamisation", but simply to enhance the powers of the

---

[33] Rudolph Peters, *Crime and Punishment in Islamic Law: Theory and Practise from the Sixteenth to the Twenty-first Century*. (Cambridge, UK: Cambridge University Press, 2005), 54.

[34] *Ibid.*

[35] See the report at http://www.themalaymailonline.com/malaysia/article/dpm-tabling-of-private-members-bill-for-upgrading-shariah-courts#sthash.4akPkFcI.dpuf. (Accessed on 5 September 2016).

[36] An example of the concerns raised and the response by the government is found at http://www.malaysia-today.net/shariah-bill-not-backdoor-to-hudud-umno-information-chief-insists/

Shariah courts as part of the efforts in the administration of Islam, the assurances do not allay the fears of the Christian community.

This is partly due to the problematic aspect of apostasy as a punishable offence under the hudud laws and Shariah. At present, we have the Shariah Courts (Criminal Jurisdiction) Act of 1965 which confers jurisdiction upon the Shariah courts to adjudicate on offences against the precepts of Islam with punishment of imprisonment for a term not exceeding *three years* or with any fine not exceeding *five thousand ringgit* or with whipping not exceeding *six strokes* or with any of the above combination.

The Bill tabled in Parliament sought to increase the present jurisdiction of the Shariah courts by removing the upper limit and ceiling of punishment by allowing the Shariah courts to dispense with matters relating to *offences against the precepts of Islam*. Unfortunately, Muslim judges in the civil courts have given a rather wide definition to the term "precepts of Islam" as encompassing matters of creed, belief, law and morals in accordance with the concept of *siyasah syari'yah*.[37]

In essence, this definition embraces the whole of Islamic life and practice over which the Shariah court would have jurisdiction. The bill also seeks to extend the penal jurisdiction of the Shariah courts by conferring powers "to pass any sentence as allowed by *Islamic law* other than the death penalty". The nature of the expression "Islamic law" is not defined. There is a certain ambiguity and generality in the expression; leaving room for unfettered discretion upon the Shariah courts, which is neither desirable nor permitted.

Further on apostasy, the problem is its fluidity and broad definition as an offence under Islamic law. Abdullahi An-Naim examines the concept and notes that the term translated from the Arabic word *ridda* literally means "to turn back". Hence, *ridda* or apostasy is reverting from the religion of Islam to *kufr* (unbelief), whether intentionally or by necessary implication.[38]

Accordingly, the Shariah scholars have listed ways in which *ridda* or apostasy may occur which includes "denying the existence or

---

[37] See the case of Sulaiman Takrib v Kerajaan Negeri Terengganu; Kerajaan Malaysia (Intervener) & Other Cases [2009] 2 CLJ 54. Affirmed by the case of Fathul Bari Mat Jahya & Anor v Majlis Agama Islam Negeri Sembilan & Anor [2012] CLJ JT(2)

[38] Abdullahi Ahmed An-Na'īm, *Islam and the Secular State: Negotiating the Future of Shari'a*, 2008 (Kindle Locations 1760-1761)

attributes of God; denying a particular messenger of God or that a messenger is truly a messenger of God; denying a principle that is established as a matter of religion such as the obligation to pray five times a day or fast during the month of Ramadan; and declaring prohibited what is manifestly permitted (halal) or declaring permitted what is manifestly prohibited (haram). Apostasy is traditionally held to apply to any Muslim who is deemed to have reverted from Islam by an intentional or blasphemous act or utterance, even when said mockingly or out of stubbornness".[39]

This broad and fluid meaning of *ridda* or apostasy has posed insurmountable problems for the church. Firstly, since there is no means by which a Muslim can change religion without having to face some sort of punishment, it presents a dilemma for those who wish to convert out of Islam by choice as well as those who practice the religion nominally or are bound by ancestry. For such people, their only recourse is before the Shariah courts as civil courts have no jurisdiction to hear apostasy cases.[40]

Secondly, their problem is compounded by the absence of positive law and procedures providing for conversion out of Islam. At present all States in Malaysia have Islamic Enactments that provide for conversion into Islam but do not have provisions and procedures for the conversion out of Islam (with the exception of the State of Negeri Sembilan). In the absence of such procedures, Shariah judges are often unwilling to declare a person an apostate (deeming the conversion as legally recognised) and state that the Shariah courts have no such jurisdiction.[41] Without these procedures, there is definitely no certainty for those who wish to leave Islam. This anomaly represents a lacuna that is inconsistent with and against the fundamental right to freedom of religion as enshrined in the Malaysian constitution.

In the case of Negeri Sembilan, there is an express provision and procedure allowing converts to leave Islam. It has, however, come

---

[39] *Ibid.*, Kindle Location 1765

[40] Following the decision of Lina Joy v the Federal Territory Islamic Council and Ors [2007] 3 AMR 693

[41] Although with the decision of Lina Joy v the Federal Territory Islamic Council and Ors, the Shari'ah courts' jurisdiction to deal with apostasy cases may be implied, the Shari'ah courts can still deny jurisdiction until and unless expressly provided as with the State of Selangor. We are however arguing beyond express provisions to having clear procedures if freedom of religion is for all persons

under criticism for the way in which it is administered.[42] By examining the process, critics have said the true intent of the provision is not to allow for conversion out of Islam but to indoctrinate and bring converts back to Islam through consultative and counselling sessions.[43] If the criticisms are any indication, such provisions also do not really resolve the plight of converts who wish to leave Islam legally.

Thirdly, it should not be forgotten that there are some Islamic enactments that expressly make apostasy a punishable offence with sentencing or other forms of punishment. For example, in the State of Sabah, there is a specific provision that makes it an offence to attempt apostasy, with detention at a rehabilitation centre for up to thirty-six months.[44] Apart from Sabah, the States of Melaka, Pahang and Perak all set apostasy or attempted apostasy as punishable.[45] In addition, the States of Johor, Pahang, Penang, Sabah, Melaka, Sarawak, Selangor, Terengganu and Wilayah Persekutuan (Federal Territory) all provide for rehabilitation centres with terms for detention.[46]

In the case of Kelantan and Terengganu, while the hudud laws are unconstitutional, punishments for four specific offences are still enforceable.[47] One of these is apostasy and it is punishable by imprisonment, deemed suitable by the Shariah court for purposes of repentance. Once there is no hope for repentance, the property of the apostate would be forfeited.[48]

---

[42] Section 119 Administration of the Religion of Islam (Negeri Sembilan) Enactment 2003

[43] See for example the critic by Mohd Al Adib Samuri & Muzammil Quraishi. 2014. Negotiating Apostasy: Application to Leave Islam in Malaysia, *Islam and Christian-Muslim Relations*. 2014. DOI: 10.1080/09596410.2014.907054

[44] Section 63 Syariah Criminal Offences (State of Sabah) Enactment 1995

[45] Section 66 Enakmen Kesalahan Syariah (Negeri Melaka) 1991, Section 9 Syariah Criminal Offences (State of Pahang) Enactment 2013, Section 13 Crimes (Syariah) (Perak) Enactment 1992

[46] See Appendix Two for reference. Also refer the case of Revathi Masoosai reported at https://www.malaysiakini.com/news/69818

[47] As these offences are not within Federal jurisdiction, the State government may choose to enforce them. Under the hudud laws, the offences are unlawful sexual intercourse, false accusation of unlawful intercourse, intoxication and apostasy.

[48] See Section 23(3) Kelantan Syariah Criminal Code (II) Enactment (1993) 2015. Cf. the provision of Section 26 Terengganu Syariah Criminal Offense (Hudud and Qisas) Enactment of 2003 which states that repentance must be within three (3) days after discovery of the act of apostasy, failing which death and forfeiture of property may result. The death penalty cannot be carried out due to the Shari'ah Courts (Criminal Jurisdiction) (Amendment) Bill 2016 which specifically excludes this form of punishment from the shari'ah courts.

We should add that apart from specific provisions for apostasy (either under the hudud laws or Islamic enactments), there are general provisions in the Islamic enactments making it an offence to insult and bring into contempt the religion of Islam, deriding or derogating the Quran and Hadith or verses of the Quran and fatwas.[49] If one agrees with the conclusion of An-Naim, that apostasy has a wide and fluid definition under Shariah, it would not be difficult to see that an apostate would also be deemed to have committed the offence of insulting or bringing contempt to Islam.

The church is now tasked with defining the rights of those who desire to leave Islam (for whatever reason) and have their conversion out of Islam legally recognised. The urgency of this question is felt all the more with the push for amendments to the Shariah Courts (Criminal Jurisdiction) Act 1965. If the act is passed, it would only open the door for Shariah courts to mete out heavier penalties in the name of divine law.

Critical Issues and Churches' Response

It is imperative for the church in Malaysia and globally to recognise the conundrum the increased practice of Shariah brings. Enforcing Islamic legislation through the coercive powers of the state (by widening the jurisdiction and authority of the Shariah court) would only reduce religious space for minorities and lead to marginalisation or oppression. The church must therefore rise to the occasion to offer concrete responses and embark on strategic actions to preserve the secular order of the country and fundamental liberties of all citizens. To that extent, the church must position herself in a manner that would enable her to contribute, if not construct, a multi-layered discourse.

This multi-layered discourse must necessarily enhance the plurality of religious thought and life through constant engagement in Christian-Muslim relations. It is all the more needed, bearing in mind that Islam is never monolithic: there are always diverse ways of understanding and interpretation within Islam. Consequently, the differences in opinion on public issues are to be expected and encouraged so that truth and common consensus may best be achieved.

But what are some questions that are in need of common consensus? Here, the perennial question of the role of Shariah

---

[49] See Appendix Three for reference

enforced by state laws as it bears on our social order, democracy and modern constitutionalism must be urgently addressed. This must be done not only from an inter-religious perspective but also intra-religiously. Unfortunately, debates and discussion on these issues in the public are often times emotive and laden with rhetoric or polemics. The quest for a rational and sustained intra-religious dialogue together with inter-religious initiatives as a mainstream endeavour is an ever challenging one.

Notwithstanding the challenge, there are already civil society organisations together with religious groups stepping forward to undertake this task. The focus is looking for balanced solutions whilst attempting to moderate competing interests, local traditions and context. This is by no means straightforward, as apart from moderating competing interests and the diversity of voices, there is implicitly a simultaneous attempt to deconstruct the state version of religion and its powerful religious bureaucracy. Doing so would require a bottom-up approach of engaging community base feelings that would eventually challenge the presuppositions and narrative of the state as well as the radical or extreme elements in society. It is a long-term strategy and one that must involve the younger and future generations.

For the church, she must prepare and harness the next generation to participate strategically in these important initiatives, while for the global church, it is crucial to mobilise support and services for the benefit of the local churches as part of her ecumenical responsibility to further the witness of Christ in this times and age. In this respect, the church must ask the question posed by the prophet Micah: what does it mean to live out our calling and fulfil the imperatives for all humanity irrespective of race and creed to uphold every truth, strive for righteousness, love mercy, seek justice and walk humbly with the Lord? (Micah 6:8).

Christian-Muslim relations must therefore move beyond evangelism and proclamation of the gospel to seek the common good in the interest of all in the context of the nation-state. In doing so, we must hold in balance the dialectics of spirituality and piety on the one hand while redeeming and reshaping the culture of life on the other. Only then will the plurality of religious thought and life flourish in multi-cultural Malaysia.

References

An-Na'īm, Abdullahi Ahmed. *Islam and the Secular State: Negotiating the Future of Shari'a*, 2008. Kindle Locations 1760-1761

Baderin, Mashood A. Administration of Justice under the Shariah, Common Law and Civil Law System: Towards a Better Understanding, Vol 2, *Malaysian Journal of Syariah and Law* 2010, 1-48

Horowitz, Donald L. The Qur'an and the Common Law: Islamic Law Reform and the Theory of Legal Change, 42 *American Journal of Comparative Law*. 1994, 543-580

Ibrahim, Ahmad. 'The position of Islam in the Constitution of Malaysia', in A. Ibrahim, S. Siddique and Y. Hussain (eds.), *Readings on Islam in Southeast Asia*. Singapore, Institute of Southeast Asian Studies, 1985, 213-220

Kamali, Mohammad Hashim. *Shariah Law: An Introduction*. Oxford, England: Oneworld Publications, 2008

Moustafa, Tamir. Judging in God's Name: State Power, Secularism, and the Politics of Islamic law in Malaysia, *Oxford Journal of Law and Religion*. 2013, 1–16

Othman, Norani. "Islam, Constitution, Citizenship Rights and Justice in Malaysia", in Birgit Krawietz and Helmut Reifeld (eds.), *Islam and the Rule of Law: Between Sharia and Secularization*. Berlin, Germany: *Konrad-Adenauer-Stiftung e.V*, 2008

Osman, M.N. 'Towards a History of Malaysian Ulama' *Working papers*, S. Rajaratnam School of International Studies. 2007

Peters, Rudolph. *Crime and Punishment in Islamic Law: Theory and Practise from the Sixteenth to the Twenty-first Century*. Cambridge, UK: Cambridge University Press, 2005

Rahman, Fazlur. *Islam*, 2nd ed. Chicago: Chicago University Press, 2002

Samuri, Mohd Al Adib & Quraishi, Muzammil. Negotiating Apostasy: Application to Leave Islam in Malaysia, *Islam and Christian–Muslim Relations*. 2014. DOI: 10.1080/09596410.2014.907054

Appendix One
List of Substantive Islamic Enactments

Laws on the Administration of Islam

Johor Administration of the Religion of Islam (State of Johor) Enactment 2003; Administration of Islamic Law (Kedah Darul Aman) Enactment 2008; Administration of the Syariah Court (State of Kelantan) Enactment 1982; Administration of the Religion of Islam (State of Malacca) Enactment 2002; Administration of the Religion of Islam (Negeri Sembilan) Enactment 2003; Administration of Islamic Law (State of Pahang) Enactment 1991; Administration of the Religion of Islam (State of Penang) Enactment 2004; Administration of the Religion of Islam (Perak) Enactment 2004; Administration of the Religion of Islam (State of Perlis) Enactment 2006; Majlis Ugama Islam Negeri Sabah Enactment 2004; Majlis Islam Sarawak Ordinance 2001; Administration of the Religion of Islam (State of Selangor) Enactment 2003; Administration of Islamic Religious Affairs (Terengganu) Enactment 2001; Administration of Islamic Law (Federal Territories) Act 1993

Islamic Family Law

Islamic Family Law (State of Johor) Enactment 2003; Islamic Family Law (Kedah Darul Aman) Enactment 2008; Islamic Family Law (State of Kelantan) Enactment 2002; Islamic Family Law (State of Malacca) Enactment 2002; Islamic Family Law (Negeri Sembilan) Enactment 2003; Islamic Family Law (State of Pahang) Enactment 2005; Islamic Family Law (State of Penang) Enactment 2004; Islamic Family Law (Perak) Enactment 2004; Islamic Family Law (State of Perlis) Enactment 2006; Islamic Family Law (State of Sabah) Enactment 2004; Islamic Family Law (State of Sarawak) Ordinance 2001; Islamic Family Law (State of Selangor) Enactment 2003; Administration of Islamic Family Law (Terengganu) Enactment 1985; Islamic Family Law (Federal Territory) Act 1984

Laws on Shari'ah Criminal Offences

Syariah Criminal Offences (State of Johor) Enactment 1997; Syariah Criminal Offences (Kedah Darul Aman) Enactment 2014; Syariah Criminal (State of Kelantan) Code 1985; Enakmen

Kesalahan Syariah (Negeri Melaka) 1991; Syariah Criminal (Negeri Sembilan) Enactment 1992; Syariah Criminal Offences (State of Pahang) Enactment 2013; Syariah Criminal Offences (State of Penang) Enactment 1996; Crimes (Syariah) (Perak) Enactment 1992; Criminal Offences in the Syarak (State of Perlis) Enactment 1991; Syariah Criminal Offences (State of Sabah) Enactment 1995; Syariah Criminal Offences (State of Sarawak) Ordinance; 2001; Syariah Criminal Offences (Selangor) Enactment 1995; Syariah Criminal Offences (Takzir) (Terengganu) Enactment 2001; Syariah Criminal Offences (Federal Territories) Act 1997

Appendix Two
Provisions for Rehabilitation Centres

States	Relevant Sections	Terms of Detention
Johore	Section 54 Syariah Criminal Offences (State of Johor) Enactment 1997	The Majlis may, *by notification in the Gazette*, appoint any place or institution to be an approved rehabilitation centre or an approved home for the purposes of this Enactment.
Pahang	Section 65 Syariah Criminal Offences (State of Pahang) Enactment 2013	The Majlis may, *by notification in the Gazette*, appoint any detention place, moral rehabilitation institution, home or centre to be an approved rehabilitation centre or an approved home for the purposes of this Enactment.
Penang	Section 54 Syariah Criminal Offences (State of Penang) Enactment 1996	The Majlis may, *by notification in the Gazette*, appoint any place or institution to be an approved rehabilitation centre or an approved home for the purposes of this Enactment.
Sabah	Section 63 Syariah Criminal Offences (State of Sabah) Enactment 1995	(1) Whenever a Muslim person by his word or conduct whatsoever intentionally claims to cease to profess the religion of Islam or declares himself to be non-Muslim, the Court shall, if it is satisfied that such person attempts to change iktikad and belief on the Islamic religion either by his word conduct, order that the person be *detained in the Islamic Rehabilitation Centre for a term not exceeding thirty-six months for rehabilitation purposes and such person be asked to repent in accordance with Hukum Syarak.*
Malacca	Section 66	(1) Apabila seseorang Islam dengan

(BM only)	Enakmen Kesalahan Syariah (Negeri Melaka) 1991	sengaja, sama ada dengan perbuatan atau perkataan atau dengan cara apa jua pun, mengaku hendak keluar dari Agama Islam atau mengisytiharkan dirinya sebagai orang yang bukan Islam, Mahkamah hendaklah, jika berpuashati bahawa seseorang itu telah melakukan sesuatu yang boleh ditafsirkan telah cuba menukarkan iktikad dan kepercayaan Agama Islam sama ada dengan pengakuan atau perbuatannya sendiri, memerintahkan orang itu supaya *ditahan di Pusat Bimbingan Islam untuk tempoh tidak melebihi enam bulan (six months) dengan tujuan pendidikan dan orang itu diminta bertaubat mengikut hukum syarak.*
Sarawak	Section 51 Syariah Criminal Offences (State of Sarawak) Ordinance 2001	The Majlis may, *by notification in the Gazette*, appoint any place or institution to be an approved rehabilitation centre or an approved home for the purposes of this Ordinance.
Selangor	Section 53 Syariah Criminal Offences (Selangor) Enactment 1995	The Majlis may, *by notification in the Gazette*, declare any place to be an approved rehabilitation centre or an approved home for the purposes of this Enactment.
Terengganu	Section 66 Syariah Criminal Offences (Takzir) (Terengganu) Enactment 2001	The Majlis may, *by notification in the Gazette*, appoint any place or institution to be an approved rehabilitation centre or an approved home for the purposes of this Enactment.
Federal Territories	Section 54 Syariah Criminal Offences (Federal Territories) Act 1997	The Majlis may, *by notification in the Gazette*, appoint any place or institution to be an approved rehabilitation centre or an approved home for the purposes of this Act.

Appendix Three
Provisions for Offences Against Insulting or Bring Contempt to Islam or Deriding or Derogating the Quran and Hadith

States	Relevant Sections	Terms of Punishments
Johore	Section 7 Syariah Criminal Offences Enactment 1997	Any person who orally or in writing or by visible representation or in any other manner - (a) insults or brings into contempt the religion of Islam; (b) derides, apes or ridicules the practices or ceremonies relating to the religion of Islam; or (c) degrades or brings into contempt any law relating to the religion of Islam for the time being in force in the State of Johor, *shall be guilty of an offence and shall on conviction be liable to a fine not exceeding three thousand ringgit or to imprisonment for a term not exceeding two years or to both.*
	Section 8 Syariah Criminal Offences Enactment 1997	Any person who, by his words or acts, derides, insults, ridicules or brings into contempt the verses of Al-Quran or Hadith *shall be guilty of an offence and shall on conviction be liable to a fine not exceeding five thousand ringgit or to imprisonment for a term not exceeding three years or to both.*
Kedah	Section 28 Syariah Criminal Offences (Kedah Darul Aman) Enactment 2014	Any person who derides or despises any law in force in Court *shall be guilty of an offence and shall be liable, on conviction, to a fine not exceeding one thousand ringgit or to imprisonment for a term not exceeding six months or to both.*
Pahang	Section 11 Syariah Criminal	Any person who orally or in writing or by visible representation or in any

	Offences Enactment 2013	other manner- (a) insults or brings into contempt the religion of Islam; (b) derides, apes or ridicules the practices or ceremonies relating to the religion of Islam; or (c) degrades or brings into contempt any law relating to the religion of Islam for the time being in force in the State of Pahang, *commits an offence and shall, on conviction, be liable to a fine not exceeding five thousand ringgit or to imprisonment for a term not exceeding three years or to whipping not exceeding six strokes or to any combination thereof.*
	Section 12 Syariah Criminal Offences Enactment 2013	Any person who, by his words or acts, derides, insults, ridicules or brings into contempt the verses of Al-Quran or Hadith *commits an offence and shall, on conviction, be liable to a fine not exceeding five thousand ringgit or to imprisonment for a term not exceeding three years or to whipping not exceeding six strokes or to any combination thereof.*
Penang	Section 7 Syariah Criminal Offences (State of Penang) Enactment 1996	Any person who orally or in writing or by visible representation, or in any other manner- (a) insults or brings into contempt the religion of Islam; (b) derides, apes or ridicules the practices or ceremonies relating to the religion of Islam; or (c) degrades or brings into contempt any law relating to the religion of Islam for the time being in force in the State of Penang, *shall be guilty of an offence and shall on conviction be liable to fine not exceeding three thousand ringgit or to imprisonment for a term not exceeding two years or to*

		both.
	Section 8 Syariah Criminal Offences (State of Penang) Enactment 1996	Any person who, by his words or acts, derides, insults, ridicules, or brings into contempt the verses of Al - Quran or Hadith *shall be guilty of an offence and shall on conviction be liable to a fine not exceeding five thousand ringgit or to imprisonment for a term not exceeding three years or to both.*
Sabah	Section 53 Syariah Criminal Offences Enactment 1995	Whoever derides, criticizes or mimics by words or deed or insults or performs an act which causes any verses of the Quran or Hadith to be put under situation or place which tarnishes the said Holy Quran or Hadith or word connected to the religion of Islam *shall be guilty of an offence and shall, on conviction, be liable to a fine not exceeding two thousand ringgit or to imprisonment for a term not exceeding one year or to both.*
	Section 54 Syariah Criminal Offences Enactment 1995	Whoever by words or dead teases, mimics or makes fun of the teaching or rites relating to the religion of Islam *shall be guilty of an offence and shall, on conviction, be liable to a fine not exceeding five thousand ringgit or to imprisonment for a term not exceeding three years or to both.*
	Section 55 Syariah Criminal Offences Enactment 1995	(1) Whoever by words spoken or written or by visible representation or in any other manner which insults or brings into contempt or ridicule the religion of Islam or the tenets of any lawful school or any lawfully appointed religious officer, religious teacher, Imam, any lawfully issued fatwa by the Majlis or the Mufti under the provisions of any law or this Enactment *shall be guilty of an offence and shall, on conviction, be liable to a fine not exceeding two thousand ringgit or to imprisonment for a term not*

			exceeding one year or to both. (2) A Muslim who claims that he is not a Muslim *shall be guilty of an offence under subsection (1) and shall, on conviction, be liable to the punishment thereunder provided.*
Malacca (BM only)	Seksyen 61 Enakmen Kesalahan Syariah (Negeri Melaka)		Sesiapa yang mempermainkan, mencela, mengejek-ejek dengan perkataan atau perbuatan atau menghina al-Quran atau Hadith Nabi atau perkataan yang berkaitan dengan Agama Islam *adalah merupakan suatu kesalahan dan apabila disabitkan kesalahan boleh dikenakan hukuman denda tidak melebihi lima ribu ringgit atau dipenjara selama tempoh tidak melebihi tiga puluh enam bulan atau kedua-duanya sekali.*
	Seksyen 62 Enakmen Kesalahan Syariah (Negeri Melaka)		Sesiapa yang mengolok-olok, mengajuk atau mengejek-ejek akan Agama Islam, dengan perkataan atau perbuatan atau amalan atau upacara yang berkaitan dengan Agama Islam *adalah merupakan suatu kesalahan dan apabila disabitkan kesalahan boleh dikenakan hukuman denda tidak melebihi lima ribu ringgit atau dipenjara selama tempoh tidak melebihi tiga puluh enam bulan atau kedua-duanya sekali.*
	Seksyen 63 Enakmen Kesalahan Syariah (Negeri Melaka)		(1) Sesiapa dengan secara lisan atau tulisan atau kelakuan yang nyata atau sebarang cara yang membawa kepada mencerca atau disifatkan sebagai menghina atau cuba mencerca atau menghina Agama Islam, perjalanan mana-mana mazhab yang muktabar, pegawai Agama, Guru Agama dan Imam yang dilantik dengan sahnya menurut undang-undang, manamana fatwa yang dikeluarkan oleh Majlis atau Mufti di bawah peruntukan Enakmen ini, *adalah merupakan suatu kesalahan dan apabila*

			disabitkan kesalahan boleh dikenakan hukuman denda tidak melebihi lima ribu ringgit atau dipenjara tidak melebihi tiga puluh enam bulan atau kedua-duanya sekali. (2) Seseorang Islam yang mendakwa dirinya sebagai seorang bukan Islam *adalah merupakan suatu kesalahan dan apabila disabitkan kesalahan mengikut subseksyen (1) seksyen ini kerana mempersendakan Agama Islam dan apabila disabitkan kesalahan boleh dikenakan hukuman yang diperuntukkan dalamnya.*
Negeri Sembilan	Section 49 Syariah Criminal (Negeri Sembilan) Enactment 1992	Any person who derogates, insults, derides or put in contempt either in words or acts the verses of the Al-Quran or Hadith *shall be guilty of an offence and shall be liable on conviction to a fine not exceeding five thousand ringgit or to an imprisonment for a term not exceeding three years or to both.*
	Section 50 Syariah Criminal (Negeri Sembilan) Enactment 1992	Any person who by words, either spoken or written, or by signs, or by visible representation, or by any act, activity or conduct, or otherwise in any other manner- (i) insult, or deemed as putting into contempt or attempt to insult or putting into contempt the Religion of Islam; or (ii) derogate, ape or derides the practices or ceremonies relating to the Religion of Islam; or (iii) the conduct of any of the recognised (muktabar) mazhab; or (iv) any fatwa legally issued by the Mufti under the Administration of the Islamic Law (Negeri Sembilan) Enactment 1991 [En. 1/1991], *shall be guilty of an offence and shall be liable on conviction to a fine not exceeding*

		five thousand ringgit or imprisonment for a term not exceeding three years or to both.
Perak	Section 14 Crimes (Syariah) Enactment 1992	Anyone who by words, either spoken or written, or by signs, or by visible representation or by any act, activity or conduct, or otherwise in any other manner- (i) insults, or is deemed to bring into contempt or attempts to insult or bring into contempt the Religion of Islam; or (ii) derides, apes or ridicules the practices or ceremonies relating to the Religion of Islam, *commits an offence and shall, on conviction, be liable to a fine not exceeding three thousand ringgit or to imprisonment for a term not exceeding two years or to both.*
	Section 15 Crimes (Syariah) Enactment 1992	Anyone who derides, insults, ridicules or brings into contempt by his words or acts the Quranic verses or Hadith *commits an offence and shall, on conviction, be liable to a fine not exceeding five thousand ringgit or to imprisonment for a term not exceeding three years or to both.*
	Section 17 Crimes (Syariah) Enactment 1992	Anyone who degrades or brings into contempt any law relating to the Religion of Islam in force in the State of Perak Darul Ridzuan *commits and offence and shall, on conviction, be liable to a fine not exceeding three thousand ringgit or to imprisonment for a term not exceeding two years or to both.*
Perlis	Section 37 Criminal Offences in the Syarak Enactment 1991	(1) Whoever, whether orally or in writing or in any manner whatsoever, treats with contempt or causes to be treated with contempt, the Quran, any ayat from the Quran or any hadis or any word or ayat that is regarded

			as holy according to the Hukum Syarak or any act or ceremony which is connected with the Religion of Islam, *shall be guilty of an offence and shall be liable, on conviction, to a fine not exceeding five thousand ringgit or to imprisonment for a term not exceeding three years or to both.*
			(2) For the purpose of sub-section (1) "treat with contempt" includes to insult, deride, mock, abuse, curse or make fun of.
		Section 39 Criminal Offences in the Syarak Enactment 1991	Whoever, whether orally or in writing or by any act or in any manner whatsoever, treats with contempt the religion of Islam or any fatwa which is lawfully issued under the Administration of Muslim Law Enactment, 1963, *shall be guilty of an offence and shall be liable, on conviction, to a fine not exceeding three thousand ringgit or to imprisonment for a term not exceeding one year or to both.*
			[Section 43 defines "treat with contempt" as including "to insult, deride, mock, abuse, curse or make fun of".]
	Sarawak	Section 7 Syariah Criminal Offences Ordinance 2001	Any person who orally or in writing or by visible representation or in any other manner-
			(a) insults or brings into contempt the religion of Islam;
			(b) derides, apes or ridicules the practices or ceremonies relating to the religion of Islam; or
			(c) degrades or brings into contempt any law relating to the religion of Islam for the time being in force in the State,
			shall be guilty of an offence and shall on conviction be liable to a fine not exceeding three thousand ringgit or to imprisonment

			for a term not exceeding two years or to both.
		Section 8 Syariah Criminal Offences Ordinance 2001	Any person who, by his words or acts, derides, insults, ridicules or brings into contempt the verses of Al-Quran or Hadith *shall be guilty of an offence and shall on conviction be liable to a fine not exceeding five thousand ringgit or to imprisonment for a term not exceeding three years or to both.*
Selangor		Section 9 Syariah Criminal Offences (Selangor) Enactment 1995	Any person who derides, insults, ridicules or brings into contempt by his words or acts the verses of Al-Quran or Hadith *shall be guilty of an offence and shall be liable on conviction to a fine not exceeding five thousand ringgit or to imprisonment for a term not exceeding three years or to both.*
		Section 10 Syariah Criminal Offences (Selangor) Enactment 1995	Any person who by words which are capable of being heard or read or by drawings, marks or other forms of representation which are visible or capable of being visible or in any other manner- (a) insults or brings into contempt the religion of Islam; (b) derides, apes or ridicules the practices or ceremonies relating to the religion of Islam; or (c) degrades or brings into contempt any law relating to the religion of Islam for the time being in force in this State, *shall be guilty of an offence and shall be liable on conviction to a fine not exceeding five thousand ringgit or to imprisonment for a term not exceeding three years or to both.*
Terengganu		Section 8 Syariah Criminal Offences (Takzir) (Terengganu)	Any person who orally or in writing or by visible representation or in any other manner-

	Enactment 2001	(a) insults or brings into contempt the religion of Islam;
		(b) derides, apes or ridicules the practices or ceremonies relating to the religion of Islam; or
		(c) degrades or brings into contempt any law relating to the religion of Islam for the time being in force in the State of Terengganu,
		shall be guilty of an offence and shall on conviction be liable to a fine not exceeding three thousand ringgit or to imprisonment for a term not exceeding two years or to both.
	Section 9 Syariah Criminal Offences (Takzir) (Terengganu) Enactment 2001	Any person who, by his words or acts, derides, insults, ridicules or brings into contempt the verses of Al-Quran or Hadith *shall be guilty of an offence and shall on conviction be liable to a fine not exceeding five thousand ringgit or to imprisonment for a term not exceeding three years or to both.*
Federal Territories	Section 7 Syariah Criminal Offences (Federal Territories) Act 1997	Any person who orally or in writing or by visible representation or in any other manner-
		(a) insults or brings into contempt the religion of Islam;
		(b) derides, apes or ridicules the practices or ceremonies relating to the religion of Islam; or
		(c) degrades or brings into contempt any law relating to the religion of Islam for the time being in force in the Federal Territories,
		shall be guilty of an offence and shall on conviction be liable to a fine not exceeding three thousand ringgit or to imprisonment for a term not exceeding two years or to both.
	Section 8 Syariah Criminal Offences	Any person who, by his words or acts, derides, insults, ridicules or

	(Federal Territories) Act 1997	brings into contempt the verses of Al-Quran or Hadith *shall be guilty of an offence and shall on conviction be liable to a fine not exceeding five thousand ringgit or to imprisonment for a term not exceeding three years or to both.*

The development of syariah law in Malaysia: Implications for Muslims and Christians

Dr John Cheong

Introduction

Globally, Malaysia enjoys a reputation as a multi-cultural Muslim country, where Islam is considered moderate and progressive. In light of Malaysia's implementation of syariah laws (or what I term syariazation), this article shall examine whether such acclaim is still deserved.[1] It will not detail Islamic law, *fiqh* (Islamic jurisprudence), or delve into Quranic/Hadith exegesis. Rather, this paper will discuss syariazation in Malaysia's history; its transition into modernity, its effect on its multiethnic and religiously plural citizenry; and assess its notion as the best (religious) law for everyone, including its impact on Christianity. Implications for the Malaysian Church to capably engage these realities are proposed.

A. Syariazation in Malaysia's pre-independence history

Islam arrived in Malaysia around the eleventh century via Indian Sufi and Arab missionaries and expanded through their intermarriages to local women (Milner 2008:40-41). The Malaccan empire was an Islamization watershed as these influences familiarised the locals with Muslim practices (Abdul Hamid 2002:470-471). During this period, *kadi*s (Islamic judges) are mentioned though evidence of their authority to enforce Islamic law is ambiguous (Milner 1988:24-26, 29).[2] Much of syariah was orally transmitted and decided rather than codified (Hefner 2011); the

---

[1] I use the Malaysian rendering of 'syariah' as opposed to shari'a/shariah, referring to a set of laws and regulations that administer Islam and Islamic law. Theologically, it is God's guidance for a complete Islamic way of life (Kamali 2008:2-7); anthropologically, it is a "'total discourse' [where] all kinds of institutions find simultaneous expression: religious, legal, moral and economic" (Hefner 2011:11 citing Messick).

[2] It is ambiguous because indigenous materials can "seldom be dated with accuracy" and "recensions of indigenous sources" occur in the later historical annals (Milner 1988:24, 48). Thus, modern Muslims who rely on textual sources as proof of syariah's *daily* presence tread on tenuous grounds.

reality of the law was "not in the texts but in indigenous laws" (Hooker 1988:166).

The pre-colonial Islamic legal milieu was also characterized by a multiplicity of systems, with no fixed authoritative body of law, no set of binding precedents and no single legitimate way of applying or changing them (Yahaya 2015:507-508). Historically, three streams of laws were practiced: *Hukum Syarak (Shara')*, which is the body of laws derived from divine or Quranic sources which the British later termed "Muhammadan laws"; *adat perpateh* (the widely patriarchal Malay tradition); and *adat temenggong* (the matriarchal Minangkabau tradition) (Mohamad 2011:3).

When the term *sharia* was used, it "was not usually invoked as the sole source of law [as] adat was frequently given equal status".[3] When it is mentioned, its application was "limited to the urban elites in the cities" (Chee, Jones and Mohamad 2009:4) and confined primarily to matrimonial and commercial matters. Where criminal law is concerned, "Islamic penalties are suggested only as alternatives to the customs of the land" (Milner 1988:27); the effectiveness of these systems of law depended much on the ruler's discretion (Milner 1988:43, Peletz 2002:29).[4] It was this "non-institutional and non-legalistic version of the doctrine [that] many S.E. Asian Muslims ... take to be Islam" (Hooker 1988:162).

Islamization and the rise of the syariah-minded became more popular in the late Ottoman empire, when the Sultan's aura and authority were eroded by British colonialism and the advent of modernity. Colonialism limited and interfered in the sultans' prerogatives (notwithstanding the British 1874 Pangkor Treaty that supposedly demarcated the boundary of authority between the colonialists and the sultans). In some cases, the sultans initiated British involvement (Mohamad 2011:4). More significantly, their interference occurred at the behest of Arab Muslim migrants in the colony who desired to circumvent the *kadis*' authority when Arab interpretations of Islam conflicted with local Muslim laws on intermarriages with Malay women (Yahaya 2015).

From 1875 to 1895, Muslim law developed into a system of rules that were "rationalizations of what the courts took to be the law and

---

[3] Abdul Hamid (2002) disputes this syncretism of syariah law and adat. However, Mohamad (2009) and Peletz (2002:228; 2015) assert this exists.

[4] See also Peletz (2002:30-37) for local rulers' variation in enforcing punishments.

custom of local Muslims ..." (Hooker 1988:170). This was formulated into the first statutory law for Muslims – the Mahomedan Marriage Ordinance of 1888 (Mohamad 2011:4-5).

Up until Malaysia's pre-independence period, one tension that prevailed was that of *Hukum Syarak* vis-à-vis *adat*. For example, tussles occurred when male litigants invoked *Hukum Syarak* to establish their right to land inheritance over female adat rights or when the Malay ruling class deployed them to mitigate the adat authority of local leaders (ibid.:5-8).[5]

Tensions between law and *adat* also emerged when the sultans "initially opposed any declaration installing Islam as the established religion of the Federation, for they feared such an enactment would transfer any authority they wielded as heads of Islam in their own states to the proposed Head of the Federation. The sultans finally relented after the Alliance explained to them that the purpose of making Islam the official religion was 'primarily for ceremonial purposes' (Abdul Hamid 2009:160). To resolve this, postcolonial leaders upheld the colonial legal framework that syariah would not be the law for all citizens or even the whole law for Muslims, an arrangement "not unique to Malaysia" (Aljunied 2016:132).

B. Syariazation in Malaysia's post-colonial period

Post-independence, Malaysia's constitution upheld the civil court's primacy in the form of the Federal Court while the syariah courts remained under the jurisdiction of the State and were applicable for Muslims only (Wan Muhammad 2011:246). In the 1970s, an Islamic resurgence fueled the later passage of many legislative measures that established state syariah courts and various enactments for administering Islamic law (Chee, Jones and Mohamad 2009:6). In 1984, the passing of the Federal Territory Administration of Islamic Laws created a multifold Islamic bureaucratic expansion almost overnight (Mohamad, Aziz and Chin 2009:66). However, Malaysia's court system was split as it resulted in fourteen sets of Islamic family laws. Contradictions also arose from the parallel jurisdiction of the syariah court system at the state level and the civil court at the federal level (Abdul Hamid 2009:163). Conflicts occurred when Muslims appealed marital cases

---

[5] Malay adat recognizes *harta sepencarian*, the equal division of estate between male and female heirs and was "consistently proclaimed by *kadi* and *ulamas* to be in consonant with *Hukum Syarak*, even though this tradition was not present in other Muslim societies outside of the Malay world" (Muhammad 2011:10).

at the federal level after the syariah courts' decisions and the civil court quashed the latter's rulings (Wan Muhammad 2011:249). This situation prevailed until 1988 when article 121 in the Federal Constitution was amended and a new clause, 1(A) was inserted, stating the Federal Court "shall have no jurisdiction in respect of any matter within the jurisdiction of the Syariah Courts".[6] However, as we shall later see, this amendment does not fully resolve the contradictions.

Other measures enacted included the increased jurisdiction of syariah courts to decide on apostasy and new Islamic family laws.[7] Indeed, "state Islamization can be traced largely to the expansion of the Islamic bureaucracy and the Syariah Court system" (Mohamad, Aziz and Chin 2009:64).

Table 1: Legislative reforms and the expansion of the Islamic bureaucracy[8]

Year	Enactments	Significance
1952	Administration of Islamic Laws (Selangor)	First piece of legislation which established the manifest place of syariah in a nascent post-colonial Malaysia.
1953-1974	Administration of other Islamic laws in other states	Post-colonial process of entrenching Muslim laws.
1984	Federal Territory Administration of Islamic Laws	Substantial centralization and augmentation of syariah system. Paved way for more uniform set of Muslim laws. Legislation also empowered and enlarged the syariah court system.

---

[6] Though many interpret this to mean "jurisdictional dualism" others believe this is 'misconceived' as "nothing in the Federal Constitution suggests that the Syariah Court is to compete with or be parallel to the civil court on the same subject matter" (Dahlan and Sabila Faudzi 2015:10). Ahmad Ibrahim's sophisticated counterargument is that Article 3 in Malaysia's constitution "entitles Muslims 'to lead their way of life according to the teachings of Islam' and that 'if [they] wish to follow the Islamic law rather than the Common Law, they should be allowed to do so" (Lee 2010:79). In addition, the constitution "cannot affect the validity of the Shariah which is non-written and is certainly not passed after Merdeka Day" (ibid.:80).

[7] On the long march towards the desecularization of Malaysia's social and legal systems, see Peletz (2015:492).

[8] On the different phases of syariazation, see Mohamad, Aziz and Chin (2009:65-66) and Mohamad (2015).

| 1988 | Addition of Clause 1A in Article 121 of Malaysia's constitution | Formalized a parallel system of laws and its administration by syariah courts. Muslims are legally bound to settle all legal matters codified under their respective state syariah laws. |

Notwithstanding these institutional restructurings, a new Islamic politico-legal elite salaried by the government and a vocal Islamic civil society resulted and began representing the conscience of this new and empowered Islamic state bureaucracy (Mohamad, Aziz and Chin 2009:66). However, because these elites were government clients, their views were tolerated only up to the point where their presence was just enough to legitimize the established order (Abdul Hamid 2009:170). The fatwas were vulnerable to political manipulation and arbitrary judgment by mufti and the state appointed client's positions that favoured only the Sunni Shafi'i school (Abdul Hamid 2009:185). We shall shortly examine how these dynamics introduced other complications.

So entrenched is Islamization and syariazation today that "key debates among Malay political and religious elites concern not whether Malaysia is (or should become) an Islamic state but what kind of Islamic state it *already* is and what types of additional measures are needed to entrench that status" (Peletz 2015:493).[9]

C. Malaysian Islamic reasons for establishing syariah law

Before discussing the conundrums that syariazation introduces, let us observe four reasons why Muslims may see it as important.

Recovers Islam's pre-colonial status: Islam has typically preferred the fusion of state and religion while the West prefers its separation. Malaysia's Islamists believe it "would have achieved Islamic status if not for the interference of the colonial masters and the arrival of non-Muslims" (Mohamad, Aziz and Chin 2009:99). Indeed, the current Islamic resurgence worldwide indicates great popularity among Muslims for syariah to infuse and inform the state with a modernistic garb (Hefner 2011, Peletz 2015).

---

[9] On how the UMNO-dominated government avers Malaysia has fulfilled conditions of being an Islamic state, see Lee (2010:53). On the three differing visions of Malaysia as a secular state by constitutionalists, or an Islamic state by UMNO or PAS, see Lee (2010:60).

Restores the akidah/Muslim faith: When the British ruled Malaysia, it was not uncommon to see urban Muslims consume alcohol or intermingle openly with women. Amongst the rural Malays, *joget* (a traditional Malay dance), the *kebaya* (a body-hugging blouse), *wayang kulit* (a shadow puppet play with Hinduistic elements) or the *bomoh/pawang* (traditional medicine man/shaman) were popular. One motivation of Muslim revivalists was to purify Islam from accretions of religious superstition or adat that were considered un-Islamic (Mohamad 2008, Peletz 1993).

Opposes anti-Islamic beliefs: In the 1950s, syariah was implemented to punish Muslim sympathizers of communism (Wan Muhammad 2015:33-34). Toward the late 1980s and 1990s, syariah law targeted new issues. The first was covert Christian proselytization. The Prime Minister's Islamic Religious Department proposed to ban the *Alkitab* translation of the Bible due to "fear in the minds of some Muslims that [use of the] *Alkitab* is a deliberate attempt... to proselytize Muslims" (CANews 1987:3). The second was punishing non-Sunni Shafi'i teachings by so-called deviant sects such as Darul Arqam and Ayah Pin (Mohammad 2008). Lately, the *Alkitab* (recycling the same accusations of covert proselytization) has again been targeted by banning the use of Allah to refer to God even though non-Muslims are not subject to syariah laws.

Is a reflection of the burgeoning Muslim demography: Lastly, the objective of making Malaysia an Islamic state is rationalized on the grounds of the demographic preponderance of Muslims as a contemporary fact (Lee 2010:61).

D. The conundrums of syariazation in Malaysia

When syariazation proceeded in the 1980-1990s, areas once considered secular became Islamized across the board, from personal family law (e.g, marriage, child custody) to banking and the workplace (Sloane-White 2011). When conflicts arose between syariah law and civil law, the former often triumphed. In the social-legal arena, there were three areas of conflict: (1) *adat* versus syariah law, (2) litigations involving religious conversion and interreligious marriage disputes and (3) applications to leave Islam. Due to textual capacity, only the first and second are examined.[10]

---

[10] There are other conflicts between syariazation and adat which space does not permit elaboration, e.g., against Malay spirit beliefs and ritualistic healing performances (Mohamad 2015:10, 14f, Hoffstaedter 2014:254-262, Peletz 2002:224-229).

Conflicts in the syariazation of Malay kinship culture

As noted earlier, battles between the syariah-minded and *adat*-keepers are evident in Malaysia's history. In 1951, Rembau (a Negeri Sembilan town) underwent an '*adat* crisis' when Minangkabau Muslim women opposed "legislative infringement on their inheritance rights or other customary prerogative" (Peletz 2002:58). When *adat* such as Minangkabau monogamy and matriarchal authority clashed with Islam, the latter eroded them (Mohamad 2011:4). These measures "alienated significant numbers of ordinary, especially rural, Malays, who perceive them as direct attacks on their basic values and key features of their cultural identities" (Peletz 2002:11).

When *adat* encourages couples to live with the wife's family, "Islam says that the wife should follow the husband" (ibid.:210). This is because "extended kinship is believed to …interfere with the development of the seamless brotherhood enjoined on all Muslims as members of the global Muslim community, which is … a highly valued form of family" (Peletz 2002:207-208). Conflicts also continue when Islam de-recognizes the informal adoption of children that are frequent among rural Malays (ibid.:213). All these are problematic because the Malays "differentiate themselves from one another on the basis of their *adat*, since Islam, in their view, is essentially the same wherever it is found. To grind down and obliterate distinctions of *adat* is to render Kelantanese Malays equivalent to Negeri Sembilan Malays, Javanese and Minangkabau (ibid.:231).

Lastly, "the more the syariah courts adhere to what are regarded as authentically Islamic and modern practices that entail the refashioning of new Malay-Muslim identities [that are subjective], the more they contribute to the production of a Malay-Muslim citizenry whose subjectivities and forms of kinship converge with those of the … non-Muslim[s]" (Peletz 2002:206). This refashioning "implicates the courts in the erasure of the very cultural difference they are supposed to safeguard with all of the resources at their disposal" (ibid.).

Conflicts in the syariazation of Malay marriages

When the Selangor Islamic Family Law of 1984 was first enacted, there was a progressive clause to restrict polygamy (in Section 23): the proposed marriage "will not directly or otherwise lower the standard of living that his …wives and dependents have enjoyed"

(Mohamad 2011:11). After 2000, the Family Law statutes of the 1980s were replaced by legislation enhancing men's entitlements and curtailing women's rights. What angered women was a clause which allowed for polygamy without the man having to prove the marriage was both necessary *and* just. Thus, polygamy could even be "granted to men with very little financial means" and promote inequality between wives (ibid.:13). The current Islamic Family Law Act contains other provisions that discriminate against Muslim women. These include (Anwar and Rumminger 2007:1533-1534): (1) a lower minimum age of marriage for women than men, (2) regardless of age, a woman can only marry with her guardian's consent, whereas a man need not do so, (3) a Muslim man can marry a non-Muslim woman but a Muslim woman cannot marry a non-Muslim man, (4) a man may marry up to four wives but women can only have one husband, (5) a woman is supposed to obey her husband. Her failure to comply with the "lawful" wishes of her husband means she can lose her right to maintenance.

Ironically, as men are given more leeway in family marriage laws, many petitioners in the courts are females suing for legal redress of their rights due to male negligence (Mohamad 2011:14). Sadly, such are promulgated in spite of the Egyptian Grand Mufti's opinion that the Qur'an views monogamy as the ideal form of marriage in Islam and that Abdullah Yusuf Ali's widely used English translation holds the same view (Anwar 2005:239).[11]

Conflicts in the syariazation of interreligious marriages

Though Article 121(3) was supposed to simplify legal decisions concerning Muslim matters, it complicated interreligious marriages when their spouse was a non-Muslim (see Table 2):

Table 2: Examples of syariah law complicating non-Muslim affairs[12]

Non-Muslim petitioner	Significance
Shamala	Petitioner married as a Hindu but husband later converts to Islam, then converts two sons to Islam

---

[11] However, in the 1989 edition of his translated Quran, Ali's commentary on the verse on polygamy, in which he says that the ideal and original state of marriage in Islam is monogamy "has been deleted" (Anwar 2005:239).

[12] For further details, see http://www.ccmalaysia.org/news/constitution/20051228press_statement.htm and Mohamad, Aziz and Chin (2009:77-89, 98).

	without her permission. Petitioner fights for custody of two sons but syariah court rules against her.
Subashini	Petitioner married as a Hindu under civil law but husband later converts to Islam, then dissolves marriage under Syariah Court. Petitioner files under the civil court but Federal Court dismisses her application.
Kaliammal Sinnasamy	Syariah Court decides the petitioner's husband validly converted to Islam without her knowledge. Upon his death, wife petitions to bury him with Hindu rites but civil court defers to syariah courts.

When a spouse's religious adherence is in question, children are torn from their parents or converted to Islam without prior parental consent and the syariah courts rule against the petitioners; they "do not show ...the Islamic lobby to be having a compassionate face" (Mohamad 2009:22-23).[13] In spite of such examples, vocal Muslim groups not only defended the syariah courts, they demonized the petitioners for insulting Islam or disuniting the *ummah*. Indeed, the "greatest challenge in realising Islamic law in Malaysia has been the wide perception that exists among Muslims and an increasing number of non-Muslims that the whole Islamic bureaucratic and judicial structures forego compassion and social propriety in their dealings with the public. State Islamic administrators, through their holier-than-thou attitudes, have cultivated the public image of abominable, witch-hunters and undisciplined office-bearers" (Abdul Hamid 2009:185).

In this area, Islamists commonly violate the Quranic injunction to be fair to others. Justice is "generally understood to mean 'putting everything in its rightful place', and in the context of *Shari'ah* as 'giving everyone his or her entitlement'" (Kamali 2008:199). Justice is the "one-overriding objective that characterizes the Qur'anic message as a whole [and] is a goal, not only of Islam, but of all revealed religions ... in dealing with friends or foes, Muslim or non-Muslims, all must be treated with justice" (ibid.:31).[14]

---

[13] One wonders how faithful these groups are to their ideals when the prophet Muhammad instructed judges and rulers to "Suspend the prescribed punishments ... as far as you can. For it is better to err in forgiveness than making an error in punishment" (Kamali 2008:293).

[14] See Surah 4:135, 5:8, 6:152, 16:90.

Conflict in the syariazation of non-Muslim affairs

In spite of promises by the Islamists that non-Muslims are not subject to syariah law, in reality many have been broken. Table 3 lists the many examples when Islamic authority or syariah law was applied to non-Muslims.

Table 3: Cases of syariah law extending into non-Muslim affairs[15]

Social arena	Application of Islamic authority/ syariah law	Conflicts with the non-Muslim's civil right
Church premise	Selangor Department of Islamic Affairs claims authority to raid a church in 2010.	Church civil rights are violated as syariah law cannot apply to raiding a non-Muslim premise.
Interreligious marriage	Non-Muslim converts to Islam to marry a Muslim but upon divorce, the desire to become a non-Muslim must be petitioned through syariah court.	Non-Muslim must still petition syariah court to leave Islam.
	Divorce occurs and non-Muslim spouse petitions for child custody. Syariah court rules children are now Muslim and must stay with the Muslim spouse.	Non-Muslim spouse retains little or no rights over child in violation of child custodial laws under civil laws.
Religious texts	Islamic authority denies Sikhs and Christians the right to use the term Allah in their religious texts.	Syariah law intrudes into the religious freedom of non-Muslims guaranteed under Article 11 of the constitution.

In light of these examples, non-Muslims now doubt many Islamist promises. In fact, non-Muslims must beware the Islamists warning that "when the time comes, [syariah] laws will be extended to all non-Muslims" (Marshall 2005:10). Muslims and non-Muslims within Malaysia now seriously question the legitimacy of their country's claims to be a model Islamic state in light of syariazation's many problems in the last thirty years. Last but not

---
[15] See Mohamad, Aziz and Chin (2010), Mohammad (2011).

least, the status of non-Muslims as minorities in Muslim-majority Malaysia is hardly discussed, especially when syariah law will apply to them in the not-too-distant future. This is problematic because the "primary challenge to an Islamic state is that substantive Islamic law concerning non-Muslims, as developed by classical scholars, treats non-Muslims as subjects with inferior political, legal and religious rights" (el-Gaili, cited by Lee 2010:96). Thus, unless Malaysia's Muslim authorities can fully address the issue of non-Muslim dhimmi status under syariah law and hold honest discussions with them concerning their shared future as citizens in a plural nation, they risk diminishing Islam as a religion of justice and respect, instead generating fear and mistrust among non-Muslims.

E. Christian witness in context of syariazation in Malaysia

Christian engagement with syariazation entails understanding the progressive Muslims and their opponents, the Islamists. The following is a proposed engagement based upon Jesus' incarnational ministry. Jesus' example is highlighted due to the parallels of being a minority community living under hostile religious authorities.

Jesus loved others deeply. A starting local theology is that of neighbourology (Batumalai 1995). Deep neighbourology involves not only knowing the name of others but also genuinely attempting to understand their culture and beliefs. The Church's task is to understand, and to dialogue with pluralistic voices within Islam to comprehend the tension of syariah law versus *adat*, the marginalization of Muslim women, injustice in interreligious marriages and other matters of injustice (see Yapp in this volume). By doing so, the Church may discover new approaches to facing Islamists. In addition, a deeper understanding of the Qur'an and Hadith is required of Christians who seek to fully engage with Muslims over the conflation of syariah as Islamic law. Christians well-versed in the Qur'an or Islamic history can help locals retrieve the rich diversity of views in Islam. Perhaps Muslims can find solutions there and engage in *ijtihad* to produce new understandings and recover the sociohistorical context of its revelation so that the textual heritage does not become detached from today's context (Anwar 2005:244-245).[16] When Islam is used as a source of public law and policy, Christians working with Muslim activists should use the progressive scholarship and the diversity of laws and

---

[16] On how to revive *ijtihad* today, see Kamali (2008:162-177).

practices in Muslim countries to open the public discourse and challenge the dominant orthodoxy by providing alternative opinions and breaking the monopoly and authority that traditional religious figures have over religious matters.

Jesus adapted his message and teaching for his audiences. Being with religious others is to also understand the language and categories of thought used within their community. History has shown how such interreligious learning became a tool of creative self-theologizing and reflection upon one's own religious heritage. For example, when Islam expanded and conquered vast swathes of the Middle East during the Ummayad Empire, Arab Christians responded by creatively constructing and explaining new understandings of the Trinity to Muslims (Griffith 2008:53-55). Compelled to learn Arabic in order to understand and speak to the Muslims, they later became skilled translators, rendering hundreds of ancient Greek classics into Arabic. Subsequently, Muslims acquired this knowledge base for the later flowering of Islamic civilization.

Can Christians work to empower and assist Muslims who suffer under unjust syariazation? If so, Christians must realize the following hurdles and opposition among Muslims and why they muffle their dissatisfactions. Key challenges include (Anwar and Rumminger 2007:1539-1540).

Being ill-informed of the Quran, Hadith or syariah laws. Due to this, Muslims abrogate responsibility of negotiating the permissible or encouraged forms of Islam to the religious authorities (Hoffstaedter 2014:259). Since the *ulama* are not at the forefront of reform, civil society groups and lay intellectuals assume leadership in reform movements, but their credentials/authority to engage with Islam publicly are questioned and undermined.

A belief that syariah law is God's law and is, therefore, infallible and unchangeable. This renders efforts towards reform to be regarded as un-Islamic. Consequently, many ordinary Muslims and legislators are afraid to publicly speak out on Islamic issues, fearing controversy or being labeled as anti-Islam and accused of questioning God's word by the extremists. Thus "no debates would transpire whenever any bill for Muslims were [sic] tabled in the legislative houses" (Mohamad 2011:14).[17] This fear extends to

---

[17] Ironically, "those who challenge and question the credentials of women's rights groups to speak on Islam themselves often do not speak Arabic and have not been traditionally educated in Islam [are the] professionals, engineers, doctors, professors and administrators

progressive scholars with the knowledge and credibility to speak out, but choose silence for fear of jeopardizing their jobs and livelihoods, invoking community hostility, and/or facing threats to their safety.

Islamist denial of the socio-historical construction of the syariah. That syariah law was constructed within specific contexts in its development and application within early and classical Islam civilization is often denied (Anwar 2005:244). This stultifies reasoning and shuts down critiques of syariah law, even when it is unjust in today's context.

Conservative training. In the traditional Islamic education most ulama are trained with an approach of *taqlid* (imitation) rather than *ijtihad*. This is also "based on the notion that the great scholars of the classical period who lived closer to the time of the Prophet were unsurpassed in their knowledge and interpretive skills" (ibid.).[18]

Underexposure to English/Western laws. Officials returning from more conservative centres of learning in the Arab world or locally tertiary institutions in Malaysia with little exposure to common law are unprepared to consider its merits and presume syariah law to be the sole option (Mohamad 2015, 174-175).[19]

Islamist harassment and threats towards critics of syariazation. When syariazation's shortcomings are reported or challenged, Islamists responded by mounting lawsuits against critics alleging defamation, blasphemy, apostasy, etc (Peletz 2015:492). This "lawfare" uses "duly enacted penal codes, its administrative law, its states of emergency ... to silence others perceived as threatening their values and interests, or those of the 'race', nation, or global Muslim community" (Peletz 2015:492).

Lack of proper shura (consultation) or ijma (consensus) with the public to deliberate on syariazation. This by itself ignores the rich Islamic legacy of arriving at a community consensus that benefits society.[20] This situation prevails due to the UMNO-PAS conflicts that have narrowed dialogue and plural discussion concerning the nature of

---

without any formal religious training. Their right to speak out, however, is not questioned ... but those who challenge these views [are]" (Anwar 2005:243).

[18] On how ijtihad was closed, see Kamali (2008:93-95). On the varieties of disagreements and pluralism in syariah, see Kamali (2008:99-121).

[19] However, Hamayotsu (2003:65) finds that syariazation was by a "new breed of Syariah officials, familiar with both Islamic and common laws and procedures".

[20] See Kamali (2008:100-101, 165-166, 221).

Islam and democratic debate among themselves and excluded non-Muslims (Liow 2007:181-182).

A final incarnational principle the Church must consider is that *Jesus challenged and exposed the sins of the oppressors*. If Malaysia is seen as a model Islamic state, the example and consequences of its syariazation contradict that. The great danger is that as syariazation proceeds towards full harmonization of Malaysia's civil law into its ambit, when injustice occurs under syariah law, *Quis custodiet ipsos custodes*?[21] In light of these multi-pronged challenges, what can Malaysian Christians do? The following proposals are suggested as a set, as the complex nature of transformation in Malaysia cannot ignore the structural dimensions of the country where ethnic remains writ large and is an important factor in its politics (Wong 2014:30).

Activism on common causes. Christians must work with Muslims to clearly articulate and expose sins of the poor and rich, without fear nor favour. Corruption, theft and adultery all fall within Christian moral concerns, not just syariah law. Happily, the Church has now emerged to become activist, protesting in public rallies and being more pro-active during elections (Chong 2014).

Alliance-building. Christians must do sufficient alliance-building and awareness-raising to build a public and legislative constituency that supports law reform when unjust bills appear such as enactments that were 'stealthily' adopted in parliament (Mohammad 2015:175).[22] Christian-Muslim cooperation becomes increasingly important "for progressive Muslims to work within the framework of Islam to advance progressive or liberal agendas [and] feel that their religion is being distorted by Islamists and politicians" (Lee 2010:97). In countries "governed by a constitutional democratic framework, public law must be opened to public debate, even if the law is made in the name of religion" (Anwar and Rumminger 2007:1542).

Accountability. A powerful system is needed to highlight abuses when Islamists deploy underhanded tactics, rouse mobs or issue death threats. Because the media is government-controlled,

---

[21] Latin, meaning "Who watchers the watchers"?

[22] Such alliance-building occurred in 2000 when the IFC (Inter-Faith Council) and others were established to advocate the return to constitutionalism and freedom of religion. However, vociferous Islamist opposition emerged and the IFC failed. For details, see Mohammad, Aziz and Chin (2009:91).

Christians should work with concerned Muslims to establish whistleblowing structures to publicize hidden agendas, to collect and give voice to marginalized voices.[23] Alternative sources of media such as blogs, YouTube, and international media to collect and immediately document to the world Islamist extremism are important (Wong 2014). If syariah is to be the code by which Muslims are to live by, the individual is admittedly required to obey the government (Sura 4:59) but he obeys the ruler on condition that the latter obeys the *Shari'ah*. This is reflected in a renowed *hadith* that "there is no obedience in sin, obedience is only in righteousness" and elsewhere that "the best form of *jihad* is to tell a word of truth to an oppressive ruler" (Kamali 2008:61-62).[24]

When syariazation becomes extreme, the public can scrutinize whether the Islamists' piety is consistent with the norms they publicly enforce upon others.

Economic sanctions. This is a seldom tried strategy in Malaysia, perhaps due to the backlash it may engender from the government. However, under extreme cases, such as when South Africans suffered under oppressive apartheid rule, global economic sanctions called by the resistance leaders eventually brought down the racist regime. Among the resistance was a noted Christian, Bishop Desmond Tutu. Because the Malaysian government understands the importance of the economy, such a strategy will not go unnoticed. Christians should carefully pray and consider whether this option is viable in Malaysia's context.

Conclusion

In this chapter, we see that syariazation leads to many unjust and unhappy outcomes. The coming future only promises more syariazation when Muslim demographics in Malaysia reach the Islamists' desired supermajority status (sufficient to enforce their desires at will without non-Muslim involvement). When that point arrives, will Malaysia descend into a failed state where syariazation becomes all-pervasive and oppressive? Two final lessons are considered here.

---

[23] For various activists strategies against syariazation, see Anwar (2005).

[24] Kamali (2008:63-64) adds that lest rulers be complacent, the "immunities against prosecution …that are enjoyed by this day by monarchs and heads of state, state assemblies and diplomats in other legal systems, are totally absent in Islamic law".

Too much Islamic injustice will lead to unexpected outcomes. How long can ordinary Malaysian Muslims continue with syariazation's assaults on their *adat*, marriage, sense of justice before significant counter reactions occur? Recent developments in Malaysia show that as "the state pushes for more laws, regulations and stipulations on homogeneity in order to govern the Muslim subject more definitively and less ambivalently [,] citizens are also going the opposite direction, pushing for more freedom of expression, pluralism and heterogeneity within Islam itself" (Mohamad 2009:24-25). However, when Islamists have emphasized "clean government and the provision of welfare services rather than state enforcement of Islamic law" they have done better (Hefner 2011:42). In Egypt and Iran, wholesale Islamization upon their populace produced a backlash. In Egypt, Muslim Brotherhood authoritarianism spawned a counter response that overthrew them in 2013. In Iran, stifling Muslim-clerical rule over three decades spurred a least a million Muslims to leave Islam (Markarian 2008).

Too much unjust Islamization leads Christians to Christ's suffering and the glory of the cross. Philippians 3:10 states, "I want to know Christ—yes, to know the power of his resurrection and participation in his sufferings, becoming like him in his death". In Malaysia, Christians still have many avenues to advocate justice when victimized by syariazation (e.g., legal challenges, activism, engaging with moderate Muslims or the voting booth. See Chong 2014). However, with the current oppressive climate, such options may no longer be as effective.

In this light, the Malaysian Church must prepare itself for increased suffering and persecution. In recent decades, Christians have reacted with a bunker mentality or migrated overseas because they have not appreciated how God's power is manifested in weakness. Here, two moments in history of divine weakness provide encouragement. In the 1960s, when Malaysia expelled missionaries and ended their visas, the Church faced a discipleship and leadership crisis. However, this event provoked Christians to develop local discipleship and leadership training structures such as the Bible College of Malaysia and Seminari Teologi Malaysia. Similarly in the 1970s, Sabah faced Islamization as thousands of indigenous Christians were converted to Islam. Stirred by the shallow Christianity there, the Sabah Theological Seminary was born, the first to train Christians in the Malay language. Since then, these bible schools have trained many hundreds of local pastors and leaders.

The lesson of Islamization or syariazation for the Church is that God's kingdom is not of this world. John 12:24 reminds us, "unless a kernel of wheat falls to the ground and dies, it remains only a single seed. But if it dies, it produces many seeds". Though Christians may see death or defeat, God uses the weak and foolish things of this world to humble the mighty (1 Corinthians 1:25-28). If Malaysian Christians can trust in God's Word, the future witness of Christianity in the nation can still shine brightly in spite of the long odds it faces.

References

Abdul Hamid, Ahmad Fauzi. 2002. The impact of Sufism on Muslims in pre-colonial Malaysia: An overview of interpretations. *Islamic Studies* 41, no.3:467-493.

—— 2009. Implementing Islamic law within a modern constitutional framework: Challenges and problems in contemporary Malaysia. *Islamic Studies* 48, no.2:157-187.

—— 2015. The hudud controversy in Malaysia: Religious probity or political expediency? *Southeast Asian Affairs* 2015:205-219.

Aljuneid, Syed Muhammad Khairudin. 2016. Demarginalising the sharia: Muslim activists and legal reforms in Malaysia. *ReOrient: The Journal of Critical Muslim Studies* 1, no.2 (Spring):128-146.

Anwar, Zainah. 2001. What Islam, whose Islam? Sisters in Islam and the struggle for women's rights. In *The politics of multiculturalism: Pluralism and citizenship in Malaysia, Singapore and Indonesia*, ed. Robert W. Hefner, 227-252. Honolulu: University of Hawaii Press.

—— and Jana S. Rumminger. 2007. Justice and equality in Muslim family laws: Challenges, possibilities, and strategies for reform. *Washington and Lee Law Review* 64, no.4:1529-1549.

Batumalai, Sandyandy. 1995. Learning the faith of my neighbours from a Malaysian perspective. *Asia Journal of Theology* 9, no.1 (April): 63-70.

CANews. 1987. Alkitab to be banned? November issue: 3.

Chee, Heng Leng, Gavin W. Jones and Maznah Mohamad. 2009. Muslim-non-Muslim marriage, rights and the state in Southeast Asia. In *Muslim-non-Muslim marriage: Political and cultural contestations in Southeast Asia*, eds. Gavin W. Jones et al, 1-30. Singapore: ISEAS.

Chong, Eu Choong. 2014. The Christian response to state-led Islamization in Malaysia. In *Religious diversity in Muslim-majority states in Southeast Asia: Areas of toleration and conflict*, eds. Bernhard Platzdasch and Johan Saravanamuttu, 290-320. Singapore: ISEAS.

Dahlan, Rosli and Fawza Sabila Faudzi. 2015. The Syariah Court: Its position under the Malaysian legal system. *Legal Herald* (May 2015):1-10.

Griffith, Sidney H. 2008. *The church in the shadow of the mosque: Christians and Muslims in the world of Islam*. Princeton, NJ: Princeton University Press.

Hamayotsu, Kikue. 2003. Politics of Syariah reform: The making of the state religio-legal apparatus. In *Malaysia: Islam, society and politics*, eds. Virginia Hooker and Norani Othman, 55-79. Singapore: ISEAS.

—— 2012. Once a Muslim, always a Muslim: the politics of state enforcement of Syariah in contemporary Malaysia. *South East Asia Research* 20, no.3:399-421.

Harding, Andrew. 2012. Malaysia: Religious pluralism and the constitution in a contested policy. *Middle East Law and Governance* 4:356-385.

Hefner, Robert W. 2011. Shari'a politics: law and society in the modern Muslim world. In *Shari'a politics: Islamic law and society in the modern world*, ed. Robert W. Hefner, 1-54. Bloomington, IN: Indiana University Press.

Hoffstaedter, Gerhard. 2014. Islamic Praxis and Theory: Negotiating Orthodoxy in Contemporary Malaysia. In *Religious diversity in Muslim-majority states in Southeast Asia*, eds. Bernhard Platzdasch and Johan Saravanamuttu, 253-267. Singapore: ISEAS.

Hooker, M.B. 1988. Muhammadan law and Islamic law. In *Islam in South-East Asia*, ed. M.B. Hooker, 160-182. Boston: E.J. Brill.

Kamali, Mohammad Hashim. 2000. *Islamic law in Malaysia: Issues and developments*. Kuala Lumpur: Ilmiah.

—— 2008. *Shari'ah law: An introduction*. Oxford: Oneworld.

Lee, Julian C.H. 2010. *Islamization and activism in Malaysia*. Singapore: ISEAS.

Liow, Joseph Chinyong. 2007. Political Islam in Malaysia: Legitimacy, hegemony and resistance. In *Islamic legitimacy in a plural Asia*, eds. Anthony Reid and Michael Gilsenan, 167-187. New York: Routledge.

Markarian, Krikor. 2008. Today's Iranian revolution: How the Mullahs are leading the nation to Jesus. *Mission Frontiers* (September-October):6-13.

Marshall, Paul. 2005. Introduction: The rise of extreme shari'a. In *Radical Islam's rules: The worldwide spread of extreme sharia law*, ed. Paul Marshall, 1-17. Landham, MD: Rowan and Littlefield.

Milner, A.C. 1988. Islam and the Muslim state. In *Islam in South-East Asia*, ed. M.B. Hooker, 24-49. Boston: E.J. Brill.

Milner, Anthony. 2008. *The Malays*. Oxford: Wiley-Blackwell.

Mohamad, Maznah. 2009. *Paradoxes of state Islamization in Malaysia: Routinization of religious charisma and the secularization of the Syariah*. ARI Research Institute Working Paper Series no.129. Singapore: Asia Research Institute.

—— 2011. *The evolution of syariah and postcolonial modernity: Embedding Malay authority through statutory law*. ISA E-symposium for Sociology. http://www.isa-sociology.org/publ/E-symposium/E-symposium-vol-1-2-2011/EBul-Aug2011-MaznahMohamad.pdf (accessed 13 June 2016).

—— 2015. Gender battles and the syariah: Translating Islamic marital law into practice in Malaysia. In *Changing marriage patterns in Southeast Asia: Economic and socio-cultural dimensions*, eds. Gavin W. Jones, Terence H. Hull and Maznah Mohamad, eds. 171-184. New York: Routledge.

Mohamad, Maznah, Zarizana Aziz and Chin Oy Sim. 2009. Private lives, public contention: Muslim-non-Muslim family disputes in Malaysia. In *Muslim-non-Muslim marriage*, eds. Gavin W. Jones et al, 59-101. Singapore: ISEAS.

Peletz, Michael G. 2002. *Islamic modern: Religious courts and cultural politics in Malaysia*. Princeton, NJ: Princeton University Press.

—— 2005. Islam and the cultural politics of legitimacy: Malaysia in the aftermath of September 11. In *Remaking Muslim politics:*

Pluralism, contestation, democratization, ed. Robert Hefner, 240-272. Princeton: Princeton University Press.

────── 2015. A syariah judiciary as a global assemblage: Islamization and beyond in a Southeast Asian context. In *A companion to the anthropology of religion*, eds. Janice Boddy and Michael Lambek, 489-506. New York: Wiley-Blackwell.

Sloane-White, Patricia. 2011. Working in the Islamic economy: Sharia-zation and the Malaysian workplace. *SOJOURN: Journal of Social Issues in Southeast Asia* 26, no.2: 304-311.

Wan Muhammad, Ramizah. 2011. The administration of syariah courts in Malaysia, 1957-2009. *Journal of Islamic Law and Culture* 13, no.2-3 (July-October):242-252.

Wan Muhammad, Ramizah, et al. 2015. Challenges in the enforcement of shari'ah criminal offences in Selangor: Between perception and reality. *Pertanika Journal of Social Science and Humanity* 23:31-42.

Wong, Mun Loong. 2014. Social media, power and democratisation in Malaysia: Weapons of the weak? *ISEAS Working Paper no.4*. Singapore: ISEAS.

Yahaya, Nurfadzilah. 2015. Craving bureaucracy: Marriage, Islamic law and Arab petitioners in the Straits Settlements. *The Muslim World* 105 (October):496-515.

Conclusion: Retrospect and Prospects

Dr John Cheong

In many parts of the Muslim world, a growing and popular demand for syariah law coincides with the influence of modernity and globalisation (Hefner 2011, Roy 2004). As seen in this volume, its implementation ranges from creeping change (in Malaysia), autocratic diktat (Brunei, Iran and Pakistan), top-down regional control (Indonesia) or by government fiat (Egypt).[1]

In some cases, globalisation has worsened many Muslim societies and exacerbated already existing social ills. Islamists believe the waywardness of their society would be ameliorated only if Islamic law is implemented (Peletz 2002:xiii). Another factor is post-colonial Muslim states with desires to address actors and conditions that "marginalized the *Shari'ah* [,] their own heritage and *Shari'ah*'s inability to meet their needs in the post-industrial age" (Kamali 2008:303). Generally, the concept or ideology of syariah law is

> sold to societies undergoing massive transformations and dislocations from traditional to modern, from rural to urban, and from agricultural to industrial and reeling under the impact of globalization ... It becomes appealing either as an idiom of protest or as an authentic source of faith and tradition for people who are torn away from their own religious and cultural roots and seek refuge from modern conditions of uncertainty in absolute truths (Anwar 2005:235).

While syariah is often described as Islamic law, "law" in the modern sense (pace Schumann) is too restrictive to unpack its full range. Marshall remarks that while it

> certainly gives rules and guidelines for marriage, economics and criminal law [,] it also gives guidance for spiritual and moral matters [and] this is one reason that criticism of the notion of *shari'a* often sounds strange to Muslims [thus]

---

[1] In addition to these examples, see Marshall (2005) for other ways in which syariah is introduced worldwide.

> criticizing shari'a ... as distinct from 'extreme *shari'a*, can sound like a criticism of 'justice' or 'rights' (2005:1).

On the other hand, most Muslims, when given the chance, have reacted against extreme syariah; those who advocate such laws (e.g., in Egypt, Indonesia and Malaysia) have not fared well in free elections (Marshall 2005:2). Even when they have won, they have not lasted long nationally (i.e., Egypt's Muslim Brotherhood) or survive only at the state or provincial level (i.e., Aceh in Riddell's chapter, and Kelantan and Terengganu in Yapp's essay).

However, in Islamic countries where the state has embodied or propounded Islamic values as consonant with national or human rights values, support for syariah can be subordinated "to the state's definition of the public interest, or to local custom" (Otto 2010:616) or even supporting universal human rights but simultaneously asserting local syariazation as ultimate (in C.T. and Cheong's discussion). As we conclude this volume, this chapter suggests that two major elements of the twentieth century, modernity and globalisation, can summarise how and why Muslim societies have pursued their various syariazation agendas and where they may be headed.

Modernity and syariazation

Modernity does not lessen the human religious impulse but rather drives its piety and practice toward more intense modes of personalization and bureaucratization as a legitimating tool to valorize religious values (Aupers and Houtman 2010). For example, modernity's rationalizing process fosters ever increasing forms of an aggressively homogenous literary or textual hermeneutic that is conservative and dogmatic (in Schumann's discussion) while underemphasizing its oral and lived traditions that are socially more accommodating towards ethnic and religious others (Anderson 2006:13, Peletz 2002:196-197, 232-235). In many Muslim societies, this often saddles Muslims with an impersonal and rigid religious bureaucracy that stultifies *ijtihad*. Authoritarian powers however "could offer an abstract formalism of legal certainty provided by juridical formalism that would enable the legal system to operate like a technically rational machine" (Yahaya 2015:497). However

> the structure of legal systems of developing countries ... reveals layers and fragmentation. Under the surface of the more visible present-day national laws, we find layers of legal provisions and ideologies deriving from, for example, the

socialist, authoritarian era of the 1960s and 1970s, of colonial law, of religious law, and of tribal customary law. The 'geo-legal' structure of a country, though, is far from uniform. Customary law, for example, may apply in one place, for one group, or for one particular topic, while elsewhere, for other parties or a different topic, religious law or a national law may apply instead of the customary law applied elsewhere. The layers of law differ in territorial scope, in subject matter, and in institutional set-up (Otto 2010:34).

Some "governments have ensured themselves of the support of high-ranking clerics, who have gone along with this state discourse about the beneficial incorporation of sharia" (ibid.:40). But when "Islamic scholars, who have not posited themselves as an extension of the government, have presented the incorporation of sharia as the political elite's erroneous appropriation of the power to interpret God's will, to ascertain the rules of sharia, and to administer justice accordingly ... the incorporation of sharia constitutes a marginalisation of their profession and the distortion of a good thing that has now fallen into the wrong hands" (ibid.).

Modernity has also facilitated a rising professionalized class of the syariah-minded (Muhammad 2011, Peletz 2002) towards the pursuit of certainties such as strict practices or boundaries (e.g., in the chapter on Brunei). This pursuit of certainties aligns the uncertain towards modernity's penchant for positivism (Shamsul 1995). In many Muslim societies, "the increasing importance of individual choice, and consequently of competition between advocates of different models of proper Islamic religious thought and practice [all] have the effect of raising the stakes on efforts to 'get Islam right' on the levels of both the individual and society – thus potentially also exacerbating tensions between projects for standardizing systematization and individuating processes involved in the construction of modern subjects" (Feener 2016:18).[2] Ironically, the very notion of the pious, individual Muslim subject also arose as a reaction (or desire to reclaim) one's glorious past as noted by Riddell. To do so, Islamists built on the "most compelling idea about the power of modernity brought about by Western

---

[2] Modernity however does not diminish the salience of folk/popular religions among many Muslims in India, Indonesia, Pakistan or Malaysia (Feener 2016:15). On the contrary, as formal Islam becomes more systematized, rationalized and bureaucratized, it seems to create hunger for a re-enchantment of the world from those who long for the experience of the traditional, mystical or magical. In fact, such modernizations of Islam are "extremely dislocating and otherwise deeply painful for ... all ordinary Muslims" (Peletz 2002:274).

colonization [,] its exercise in classification and the fixing of definite identities upon its constituents [such as] surveys, censuses and laws [as] exercises for categorization" (Mohamad 2011:15).

To be sure, not all blame lies with the Muslims because Western colonialism had perpetuated great injustices of its own. In Islam's present phase, syariah laws are deployed by Islamists globally as part of a protest discourse against Western colonial domination and "purports to be a project in the reclamation of an indigenous, religious-centric identity ...for the activation of its authenticity" (ibid.).

This response does not necessarily entail an extreme fundamentalism for Islam possesses many interpretations of its heritage (Kendall and Khan 2016). In some cases, this retrieval of the past may resurrect the better parts of Islam such as its creative solutions (e.g. *maqasid al-Shari'ah*) and diverse contextual interpretations (Kamali 2008:123-139). Conversely, in other cases, a number of Islamic countries ... modern Muslim family laws are grounded in assumptions that are centuries old and have little bearing on today's realities" (Anwar 2007:1536-1537). Mohammad Hashim Kamali, an Islamic law expert, however states that these laws are

> justiciable and the individual can seek judicial relief if his rights are violated by others or by the government. The rules pertaining to devotional matters, especially those which consist purely or principally of the Right of God, such as ritual prayers and fasting, etc., constitute religious obligations. Failure to fulfil these calls for moral reprimand in this world and punishment in the next, but they are basically *not justiciable* in the courts" (2008:17) [italics mine].

When progressive Muslims confront Islam's pre-modern, socio-cultural forms that are seen as ill-fitting for the twenty-first century, we witness intra-Muslim conflicts over "criminal law, the judicial system, rules of evidence, the role of women, educational systems, the media, religious freedom, and all other human rights are forced into the purported model of seventh-century Arabia" (Marshall 2005:11). On this our volume thus resonates with Jan Michiel Otto's twelve country survey of Islamic countries, that creeping syariazation has caused the most concerns when it has clashed against these areas.

In addition, when Islamists begin "endorsing a mindset that 'mainstream' Muslims are under threat and that they must be protected from 'improper' religious readings [it creates] a gap between the believer and the non-believer as individuals in religious communities no longer believe in sharing either religious practice or common values" which aids "social disturbances and legal injustice" (Platzdasch 2014:8).

In fact, increased dogmatism in syariazation often results in societies once tolerant and accepting of religious or cultural diversity now being "challenged by a contrary trend towards religious conservatism and mutual religious exclusivism, an increasing appeal of 'pure' belief models, and the resulting scepticism for local accommodations towards religious scripture and apprehension towards inter-religious mingling" (Platzdasch 2014:5).

Such problems often ensue because the historical "codification of the Syariah (since the middle of the nineteenth century) has 'brought about the transformation of the *shari'a* from the 'jurist's law', that is, a law created by independent legal experts, to 'statutory law,' in other words, a law promulgated by a national-territorial legislature" (Lee 2010:80-81). It not only fostered an ever sophisticated class of Islamic scholars capable of mining their traditions with élan; the retrieval of these traditions has been channeled by nationalist pride, anti-Western impulses and Islamic resurgence (e.g., Riddell's chapter on Egypt and Pakistan and McRoy's on Iran). Due to this, there arises among Islamists a basic impulse to totalize the implementation of syariah in both the personal and public spheres which causes great conflict both within the ummah and also between non-Muslims.

Globalisation and syariazation

In the history of the world, a dialectic between syariazation and globalisation has existed since Islam's beginning and its expansion from the Middle East to the rest of the world through globalisation's modes of commerce, conversion, conquest and intermarriages (Chanda 2007). When colonial powers with global ambitions came and dominated the Islamic world, it also encouraged global transnational connections with other Muslim powers. For instance, local ulamas not infrequently sought long-distance links to Islam's heartland to connect, borrow and integrated their systems into local Islamic traditions or syariah laws (Riddell 2001).

Other linkages were pursued to shore up local identities and sovereignty against colonialism, such as Aceh's search for Ottoman protection against the Dutch (in Riddell's essay). Often, local syariazation was strengthened by becoming more ritually strict (as in PAS in Malaysia) or militant (as in Aceh and Iran). To do so, Islamists deployed Western modern tools to establish the socio-legal edifice of syariah laws, some to the degree of amending their constitutions so that syariah law would trump or determine the substance of state laws (e.g., Aceh, Brunei, Iran and Pakistan). In this sense, syariah laws and its implementation can be said to be byproducts of global sociohistorical flows that benefitted many Islamic nations. However, it has also brought its share of conflicts.

For countries such as Malaysia, the danger is seen where syariazation feeds into the political agenda of entrenching ethnic nationalism (Mohamad 2011:1). In others (e.g., Iran, Pakistan), syariazation simply overlays, if not consolidates, already existing authoritarian norms in a religious garb. No wonder Kamali (2008:6) warns: "Declaring a state as Islamic or Shari'ah as the applied law has often co-existed with despotism and corrupt governance such that the ethical norms of Islam and its unmistakable stress on personal conduct have been conspicuously absent in the track record of the majority of Muslim political leaders of the post-colonial period".

In a globalised world, fundamentalist or radical Muslims within a nation's borders also prove alarming because the modes of globalisation allow many such small groups to access monetary funding, find ideological support through the internet and easily travel internationally to find self-empowerment (Marshall 2005:10, Yousif 2006:459). When such groups valorize syariazation as the benchmark of their cause, it has drawn many naïve Muslims to their cause célèbre. Because of this, nations such as Brunei, Indonesia and Malaysia have labeled such groups as deviant or dangerous.

Another has been the sense of victimisation and fear of Western globalisation. This often "colours their position towards religious minorities, especially Christians" (Platzdasch 2014:6). Another path is when nations responded by preserving their religious-national identities or cultures against the easing of socio-cultural, economic and religious flows facilitated by globalisation. When this occurs, "bordercrossing and the fading of borders are accompanied by the consolidation of some borders and the emergence of new ones" (Nederveen Pieterse 2002:34). "As external borders lose salience, new internal frontiers emerge, fragmenting social space by reworking existing boundaries of class and status" (e.g. ranging from ethnic and religious differences to ethnic cleansing, frontiers of class, status, consumption and style) (ibid:44-45).

Brunei for example attempts to extend its syariah laws extra-territorially (in CT and Cheong's essay) even though "it is difficult to see how its Syariah Order can be effectively implemented". For Brunei, their decision "to forge ahead with its legal Islamization policies may therefore raise the stakes in the region, particularly vis-a-vis the dynamics of 'piety-trumping' between competing Muslim political groups in Malaysia" (Müller 2016:439). If such paradoxes are at play in Southeast Asia regionally, it is likely no less true for other Islamic states globally. Conversely, globalisation has also benefitted groups like Sisters in Islam in Malaysia who can draw on the "liberal sensibilities of global feminism and transnational NGOs concerned with women's issues and human rights" (Peletz 2005:251).

When such struggles proceed without stable institutions (whether secular or religious) or the presence of strong and independent civil society groups such as NGOs and such (Otto 2010:47), syariazation tends to devolve towards greater civil strife, such as in Egypt Iran, Pakistan. Even in countries that have more or less avoided trouble (e.g., Brunei and Malaysia), it remains to be seen how long and how successful these states may avoid a similar fate.

In the larger picture, syariazation in each of our six contexts (except for Brunei) has mostly revealed many failures to temper its excesses within their *ummah*. As McRoy states, in Iran, "the visible contrast between the piety of its leaders and the incompetent handling of its economy has created a trust gap that instilled a loss of confidence in Islam as it is linked to the religious and bureaucratic competency of its state and religious authorities that are fused as one". In Brunei, syariazation seems to be in check as its speed is driven by the Sultan. However, a quiet leadership crisis potentially looms as the Sultan's successor Jeffri Bolkiah, (cited in the media as a playboy[3]) whose future ascension to the throne may delegitimize the current aura of his father and its underlying MIB ideology that underpins its entire system. Coupled with a projected depletion of Brunei's plentiful oil reserves by 2040 (The Economist 2015), the current patronage system and soft authoritarianism administered by its

---

[3] For example, see Mitton (2011) and Lauren (2010).

sultanate may have a limited lifespan. Whether this may initiate a crisis within the state or syariazation in due time will merit further attention in the coming decades.

Wither the Church under the shadow of syariah?

Today, Islam is in the midst of a great struggle between its progressive versus their conservative/fundamentalist wings. The outcome of how both sides engage one another will have enormous consequences for Christians living under their nations.

At present, as syariazation proceeds apace with little or no input from Christians or their other religious minorities in all of the countries we studied, it not only damages the credibility of Islam as a faith that is proclaimed as peaceful and tolerant, it has caused great discontent or disillusionment within its *ummah*. As Riddell notes, in Aceh's earlier history, GAM's strident goal to impose Islam in the Jakarta Charter was "crushed ... by Indonesian armed forces while in Egypt, Muslim Brotherhood authoritarianism spawned a counter response that overthrew [the Brotherhood] in 2012"; in Iran, "stifling Muslim-clerical rule over three decades spurred a least a million Muslims to leave Islam" (in my chapter on Malaysia).

As Yapp observes, for the Church, the challenge is whether in the midst of such overwhelming syariazation actors and forces, will it scurry into an individualistic, pietistic, non-public engagement burrow or realise its role as a viable agent of God's witness and love that engages the public and political arena as well? While the Church cannot do everything, it can begin with Jesus' two greatest commandments: To love God and to love one's neighbours as themselves (Matt 22:38-39). For Christians, God's clear command to love others as ourselves cannot be ignored. Christians must not only "love your enemies and pray for those who persecute you" (Matt 5:44) but to also "forgive other people when they sin against you [for] if you do not forgive others their sins, your Father will not forgive your sins" (Matt 6:14-15). We should "do to others as you would have them do to you" (Luke 6:31), and "always strive to do what is good for each other and for everyone else" (1 Thess 5:15). One way is that the Church can stand against injustice when it occurs (Mic 6:8), showing God's love towards Muslims, their nearest neighbours, especially when they are victimized by their own laws and people (in my other essay in the volume). By doing this, we are "not be overcome by evil, but overcome evil with good" (Rom 12:20-21).

Christians can also ask Muslims whether they have room to explore the origins and historical understandings of syariah together and in doing so ask why particular interpretations and understandings have become essentialised while others are rejected. Perhaps Christians may gain new friendships or conversations that can open self-examination on who speaks for Islam and syariazation and what net effect may occur in its implementation. When they do so, they will discover that Muslims are not uniform in their views on syariazation and whether it is wholly beneficial. For example, while Muslims may desire more syariah, it may not "be of the classical and static type [nor] depend on the old structures of authority" (Otto 2010:617). Even in many Muslim countries worldwide (in a thirty nine country and territory survey of across three continents), among Muslims who "support making sharia the law of the land, most do not believe that it should be applied to non-Muslims" (Pew Research Center 2013:48). Furthermore, insofar as

> those in favor of making sharia the law of the land ... [l]ower but substantial proportions of Muslims support severe punishments such as cutting off the hands of thieves or stoning people who commit adultery. The survey finds even lower support for executing apostates (ibid.:50).

Esposito and Mogahed (cited by Otto 2010:617) state that

> clear majorities of respondents throughout the Muslim world find that women should have the same legal rights as men. Generally, the support for democracy and human rights is also significant. Muslims seem to entrust key decisions in law and governance to the 'new' legal institutions of the state, rather than to the old structures of sharia authority.[4]

Lastly, if the picture may seem gloomy for Christians who live under the shadow of syariah, mere statistics or ten second news sound bites fail to tell of the many unreported stories of a deeper maturation among current believers, fortified faith among Christians and wiser biblical knowledge among its leaders and followers as a result of its being forced to engaged with syariazation worldwide. In my essay on Malaysia, I note how "God's power is manifested in weakness" resulting from Islamisation. In Yapp's

---

[4] The Pew Research Center survey (2013:99) however finds that "Muslims who favor an official role for sharia also tend to be less supportive of granting specific rights to women".

essay, we saw how Malaysia's syariah laws governing intermarriages and the banning of terms such as Allah have united the Church to defend its rights; it has also stirred more moderate Malay Muslim political bystanders to participate in civil society groups and protest against the excesses of Malaysia's Islamic authorities. If due to such unforeseen (or divinely ordained?) reasons syariazation may lead to increased freedom, future strengthening or flowering of the Church in Malaysia and worldwide, perhaps the other side of syariah's shadow hides coming rays of divine grace and sovereignty that follows it and gives Christians hope amidst syariazation's seemingly unrelenting march.

References

Anderson, Benedict. 2006 [1993]. *Imagined communities: Ethnicity, religion and nationalism*. New York: Verso.

Anwar, Zainah. 2005. Sisters in Islam and the struggle for women's rights. In *On shifting ground: Muslim women in the global era*, ed. Fereshteh Nouraie-Simone, 233-247. New York: The Feminist Press.

Aupers, Stef and Dick Houtman, eds. 2011. *Religions of modernity: Relocating the sacred to the self and the digital*. Leiden: E.J. Brill.

Chanda, Nayan. 2007. *Bound Together: How traders, preachers, adventurers, and warriors shaped globalization*. New Haven, CT: Yale University Press.

Feener, R. Michael. 2016. State shari'a and its limits. In *Islam and the limits of the state: Reconfigurations of practice, community and authority in contemporary Aceh*, eds. R. Michael Feener, David Kloos and Annemarie Samuels, 1-23. Leiden: E.J. Brill.

Hefner, Robert W, ed. 2011. Introduction. In *Shari'a politics: Islamic Law and Society in the Modern World*, ed. Robert W. Hefner, 1-54. Bloomington, IN: Indiana University Press.

Kendall, Elisabeth and Ahmad Khan. 2016. Introduction. In *Reclaiming Islamic tradition: Modern interpretations of the classical heritage*, eds. Elisabeth Kendall and Ahman Khan, 1-11. Edinburgh: Edinburgh University Press.

Kamali, Mohammad Hashim. 2008. *Shari'ah law: An introduction*. Oxford: Oneworld.

Lauren, Jillian. 2010. *Some girls: My life in a harem*. New York: Plume.

Lee, Julian C.H. 2010. *Islamization and activism in Malaysia*. Singapore: ISEAS.

Marshall, Paul. 2005. Introduction: The rise of extreme shari'a. In *Radical Islam's Rules*, ed. Paul Marshall, 1-12. Lanham, MD: Rowman and Littlefield.

Mitton, Roger. 2011. Playboy prince may live to regret his partying lifestyle. *The Phnom Penh Post*, 31 January. http://www.phnompenhpost.com/columns/playboy-prince-may-live-regret-his-partying-lifestyle (accessed 25 August 2017).

Mohamad, Maznah. 2011. *The evolution of syariah and postcolonial modernity: Embedding Malay authority through statutory law*. ISA E-symposium for Sociology. http://www.isa-sociology.org/publ/E-symposium/E-symposium-vol-1-2-2011/EBul-Aug2011-Maznah Mohamad.pdf (accessed 13 June 2016).

Müller, Dominik. 2016. Paradoxical normalities in Brunei and Malaysia. *Asian Survey* 56, no.3: 415-441.

Nederveen Pieterse, Jan. 2002. Fault lines of transnationalism: Borders matter. *Bulletin of the Royal Institute for Inter-faith Studies* 4 (2):33-48.

Otto, Jan Michiel. 2010. Introduction. In *Sharia incorporated: A comparative overview of the legal systems of twelve Muslim countries in past and present*, ed. Jan Michiel Otto, 18-49. Leiden: Leiden University Press.

—— 2010. Towards comparative conclusions on the role of sharia in national law. In *Sharia incorporated*, ed. Jan Michiel Otto, 613-654. Leiden: Leiden University Press.

Platzdasch, Bernhard. 2014. Introduction. In *Religious diversity in Muslim-majority states in Southeast Asia: Areas of toleration and conflict*, eds. Bernhard Platzdasch and Johan Saravanamuthu, 3-15. Singapore: ISEAS.

Peletz, Michael. 2002. *Islamic modern: Religious courts and cultural politics in Malaysia*. Princeton, NJ: Princeton University Press.

—— 2005. Islam and the cultural politics of legitimacy: Malaysia in the aftermath of September 11. In *Remaking Muslim politics:*

Pluralism, contestation, democratization, ed. Robert Hefner, 240-272. Princeton: Princeton University Press.

Pew Research Center. 2013. *The world's Muslims: Religion, politics and society*. Washington D.C.: Pew Research Center's Forum on Religion & Public Life. http://www.pewforum.org/2013/04/30/the-worlds-muslims-religion-politics-society-beliefs-about-sharia/ (accessed 13 July 2017).

Riddell, Peter. 2001. *Islam and the Malay-Indonesian world: Transmission and Responses*. Honolulu, HI: University of Hawaii Press.

Roy, Olivier. 2017. *Jihad and death: The global appeal of Islamic state*. London: Hurst.

Shamsul, A.B. 1995. The dakwah persona. In *The pursuit of certainties: Religious and cultural formulations*, ed. Wendy James, 112-133. New York: Routledge.

The Economist. 2015. All pray and no work: An autocratic sultanate turns more devout as oil money declines. 15 August. http://www.economist.com/news/asia/21661040-autocratic-sultanate-turns-more-devout-oil-money-declines-all-pray-and-no-work?Fsrc=rss (accessed 13 December 2015).

Yousif. Ahmad F. 2006. Contemporary Islamic movements in Southeast Asia: Challenges and opportunities. In *The Blackwell companion to contemporary Islamic thought*, ed. Ibrahim M. Abu-Rabi', 449-465. New York: Wiley-Blackwell.

Appendix One
Online resources on select
global and regional civil and shariah law codes

General legal resources:

GlobaLex. http://www.nyulawglobal.org/globalex/about.html

Pew Research Center 2013 Report. *Muslim beliefs about sharia: The World's Muslims: Politics, religion and society* (Pew Research Center): http://www.pewforum.org/2013/04/30/the-worlds-muslims-religion-politics-society-beliefs-about-sharia/

Pew Research Center 2016 Report. *The Divide Over Islam and National Laws in the Muslim World: Varied views on whether Quran should influence laws in countries*, http://www.pewglobal.org/2016/04/27/the-divide-over-islam-and-national-laws-in-the-muslim-world/

Regional resources:

Aceh: Aceh Syar'iyah Court. www.ms-aceh.go.id/

Brunei: Official website of the Brunei Syariah Court. https://www.e-syariah.gov.bn

Egypt: An Overview of the Egyptian Legal System and Legal Research.
http://www.nyulawglobal.org/globalex/Egypt.html

Indonesia: The Indonesian Legal System and Legal Research. http://www.nyulawglobal.org/globalex/Indonesia.html

Iran: A Guide to the Legal System of the Islamic Republic of Iran. http://www.nyulawglobal.org/globalex/Iran.html

Malaysia: An Overview of Malaysian Legal System and Research. http://www.nyulawglobal.org/globalex/Malaysia.html

Malaysia: Official e-syariah portal (Malaysia). http://www.esyariah.gov.my/

Pakistan: A Legal Research Guide to Pakistan. http://www.nyulawglobal.org/globalex/Pakistan.html

Contributors

Prof. Peter G. Riddell holds a PhD from the Australian National University and serves as Vice Principal (Academic) at the Melbourne School of Theology and Professorial Research Associate in the Department of History at SOAS, University of London. He previously taught at the Australian National University, the Institut Pertanian Bogor (Indonesia), SOAS and the London School of Theology, where he served as Professor of Islamic Studies. He was invited as visiting professor at L'Ecole Pratique des Hautes Etudes/Sorbonne (Paris) in May/June, 2015.

He has published widely on the study of Southeast Asia, Islam and Christian-Muslim Relations. His books include *Transferring a Tradition* (Berkeley, 1990); *Islam and the Malay-Indonesian World* (London, Hawaii, and Singapore, 2001); Christians and Muslims (Leicester, 2004); and *Malay Court Religion, Culture and Language: Interpreting the Qur'an in 17th Century Aceh* (Leiden, 2017). Among his edited volumes are *Islam and Christianity on the Edge: Talking Points in Christian-Muslim Relations into the 21st Century* (with John Azumah, Melbourne, 2013); and *The Qur'an in the Malay-Indonesian World: Context and Interpretation* (with Majid Daneshgar and Andrew Rippin, London, 2016).

Prof. (em.) Dr. Olaf Schumann was born in Dresden, Germany. He studied Protestant Theology at the Universities of Kiel, Tübingen, and Basel (1959-1964), and Islamology in Tübingen and Cairo (*Majma' al-Azhar*) (1963-1966). He was ordained Pastor of the Lutheran Church in Schleswig Holstein (1970). He was promoted to Dr. Theology at Tübingen in 1972.

He served as Lecturer in German Language at the University of Assiut, Egypt (1966-1968). He was then appointed as Research Fellow at the Council of Churches in Jakarta (1970-1981), then Professor in Missiology and Science of Religions at Hamburg University 1981-1989 and 1992-2004. He was Guest Professor at Sekolah Tinggi Theologia Jakarta 1989-1992. After retiring in 2004 he lectured at Sabah Theological Seminary, Kota Kinabalu (Sabah/Malaysia), from 2006-2016.

Publications (selection): *Der Christus der Muslime* (1st edn. Gütersloh 1975, 2nd edn. Köln-Wien 1988, 294pp; translated into Indonesian and English); *Pendekatan pada Ilmu Agama-Agama* (Jakarta: BPK

GM 2013, 497 pp); *Filsafat & Agama* (Jakarta: BPK GM 2016, 388 pp.).

Dr Anthony McRoy, of dual UK/Eire citizenship, holds a PhD from Brunel University and is Lecturer in Islamic Studies at Union School of Theology, UK. He is the author of *From Rushdie to 7/7* (London, 2006) and has contributed to various other publications, as well as writing many articles and reviews. His research interests presently include Islamic Origins, Byzantine-Islamic relations, Shi'ism, late Ottoman relations with its Balkan, Armenian, Assyrian and ethnic Greek subjects, historical and contemporary Jihad, and current Islamic polemics. He is married with three grown up children.

Dr John Cheong holds a PhD in intercultural studies from Trinity International University, USA. He is a researcher, consultant and lecturer in missiology and teaches in various Christian colleges around Asia. He specialises in globalisation studies and Southeast Asian Islam and has published on this as well as on the cultural dimensions of economics and contextual theology. He has edited two books and published over twenty articles on the above.

Eugene Yapp holds a Bachelor of Laws (LL.B Hons), University of London; Certificate in Legal Practice (CLP), University Malaya & Malaysia Legal Qualifying Board; and a Master in Christian Studies (MCS), Malaysia Bible Seminary.

He currently serves as the Executive Director of Kairos Dialogue Network, a non-profit organisation founded upon Christian values and dedicated to the advancement of Christian-Muslim relations in Malaysia. He was formerly an Advocate and Solicitor of the High Court of Malaya and former Secretary-General of the National Evangelical Christian Fellowship Malaysia (NECF).

His publications include involvement in the preparation of the NECF *Religious Liberty Report 2008, 2009, 2010, 2011* (NECF Publications); *Transforming the Nation*, Forum VI., ed. 2007 (NECF Publications); "The 'Copyright' Controversy of 'Allah': Issues and Challenges Assailing the Malaysian Church", and "Caning Kartika! Is Religious Parochialism Growing in Malaysia?", in *The Church in a Changing World: An Asian Response: Challenges from the Malang Consultation on Globalization*, 2010 (ATA Publications).

Notes for Contributors

Submission requirements:

Manuscript

- Papers should not exceed 5000 (not including footnotes) words, although the Editor retains the discretion to publish papers beyond this length.

- It is preferable that submissions be prepared in Microsoft Word format.

- All papers are to be written in English, and an English transliteration given to any quotations or short phrases in original language.

- Authors are advised to use gender inclusive and non-discriminatory language.

- Any visuals should be integrated into the document, or sent separately as separate jpg or gif files with an explanation as to their position in the paper.

- Footnotes should follow the style used in previous issues of this Occasional Paper series. Please ensure that the first reference to any work in the footnotes includes all bibliographic detail. Also note that footnotes should constitute no more than an extra 25% of the word total. (That is 1250 words in footnotes for 5000 words.)

- All internet references need to include the date the material was cited. eg:

    http://www.nameofsite/nameofsection, cited dd/mm/yy

Submission

- Papers to be considered for inclusion are to be submitted directly to the Editor.

- Submissions are to be forwarded via electronic mail to info@jefferycentre.mst.edu.au. If submitting within Australia, a hard copy must also be posted to Arthur Jeffery Centre for the Study of Islam, PO Box 6257, Vermont Sth., Vic 3133.

- A declaration that the submitted articles are your own work and that you've acknowledged the work/s of others used in the articles in the references, etc. must be included with any submission.

- A covering letter that includes the authors' names, titles, affiliations, with complete mailing addresses, including email, telephone and facsimile numbers should be attached to the paper.

Review of Submissions

- All submissions will be sent to referees for anonymous recommendation.

- The Editor holds the right to make editorial corrections to accepted submissions.

Copyright

- The Arthur Jeffery Centre for the Study of Islam Occasional Papers series is published by the Melbourne School of Theology Press. The copyright for any published papers will remain with the author. MST publishes these papers on the following conditions:

- They do not appear elsewhere (including web pages) for 180 days from the date of publication in the Arthur Jeffery Centre for the Study of Islam Occasional Papers series.

- Whenever they are printed elsewhere (including web pages), the following notice will be included: "This article first appeared in the __ issue of the Arthur Jeffery Centre for the Study of Islam Occasional Papers series".

- We retain the right to use the paper in any Arthur Jeffery Centre publications, reprints, or in electronic form (ie. Online, CD-Rom, etc.).

- We retain the right to use a portion or description of the paper with your name in our promotional material.

- Authors are themselves responsible for obtaining permission to reproduce copyright material from other sources.

- The author will be presented with two copies of the publication.

www.ingramcontent.com/pod-product-compliance
Lightning Source LLC
Chambersburg PA
CBHW050638300426
44112CB00012B/1848